SILENTS OF THE VAMPS:

Bad Girls You Don't Know – But Should

By Jennifer Ann Redmond

SILENTS OF THE VAMPS:
Bad Girls You Don't Know – But Should
By Jennifer Ann Redmond
Copyright © 2019 Jennifer Ann Redmond
No part of this book may be reproduced in any form or by any means, electronic, mechanical, digital, photocopying, or recording, except for inclusion of a review, without permission in writing from the publisher or Author.

Published in the USA by:
BearManor Media
P O Box 71426
Albany, Georgia 31708
www.bearmanormedia.com

Paperback ISBN: 978-1-62933-479-0
Case ISBN: 978-1-62933-480-6
BearManor Media, Albany, Georgia
Printed in the United States of America
Book design by Robbie Adkins, www.adkinsconsult.com

Front cover: Alice Hollister. Photo courtesy Terry Ann Smith.
Back cover, top: 1920s Maybelline ad (excerpt) courtesy the Media History Digital Library.
Back cover, bottom: Eis and French do their Vampire Dance in The Vampire *(1913). Photo courtesy the Media History Digital Library.*

JENNIFER ANN REDMOND

*for Antonetta Tarallo (1921-1996)
with love from your Chickadee*

ROGUES GALLERY

(and by "rogues" I mean "wonderful people who helped put this together")
Linda Bucci
Thomas Carey
ALA Unit President FR01 Ginette Crosley
John Crosse
Peter Fox
Christine Leteux
Carol Peterson of *Classic Images*
Gary L. Prange
Betty Ann Redmond
Terry Ann Smith

Jennifer Ann Redmond

THE LINEUP:

Initial Appearance: Prologue vii

Alice Hollister 1
Carmen Phillips 9
Claire de Lorez 19
DeSacia Mooers 31
Edna Tichenor 41
Iva Shepard 49
Marcia Manon 59
Olga Grey 69
Rosa Rudami 79
Rosemary Theby 89
Ruth Taylor 101

Exhibit A: Selected Bibliography 109
Index 139
About the Author 146

INITIAL APPEARANCE: PREFACE

"If it's naughty to vamp the men,
Sleep each morning 'til after ten,
Then the answer is yes, I want to be bad!"
"I Want to Be Bad," Follow Thru, *1929*

The notorious "vamp" began life as the progressive, mercurial "adventuress." The opposite of the wholesome heroine, she was not young and, though unmarried and childless, certainly not virginal. The adventuress was self-reliant, immensely likeable, and appeared trustworthy. She smoked, was witty in public, succumbed to ennui when alone. The spiritual and financial assets of her victim were her only aim. She rarely missed.

Moving pictures enlarged this good girl/bad girl dichotomy to cartoonish proportions. Having a reputation wasn't enough; the woman must look abnormal, creature-like, all raccoon eyes and poisonous movements while enchanting your husband or, God forbid, father ("old men are peculiarly liable to be enmeshed in the web"). That she was almost always brunette was no accident; the fear of newly-arrived dark-haired/dark-skinned immigrants literally colored this representation of dangerous "otherness." Her clothing was often Asian-inspired. Newspapers published warning signs and checklists to educate the public. In Newark, NJ, Judge Boettner's "policettes," a female public safety squad, patrolled the streets and forcibly scrubbed the rouge off "women flirts." Caution was urged when dealing even with the debutante set, lest a "baby vamp" dig in her talons. A few offered their necks and bankbooks willingly, fledgling "sugar daddies" paving the way for 1930s "golddiggers."

Theda Bara was the queen, and actresses like Nita Naldi, Pola Negri, and Louise Glaum her co-conspirators, desired by men, dreaded by women, and gleefully imitated by schoolgirls. Every studio had a cabal, however, and the following eleven women were just as guilty . . .

Photo courtesy Terry Ann Smith.

FILE #26158: ALICE HOLLISTER

REAL NAME: Rosalie Alice Amélie Berger
DOB: September 28, 1885 - Worcester, MA
HAIR: "ebon as night" [that's "black" for us commoners]
EYES: "velvety brown"
WANTED FOR: incitement of imminent lawless action
ON THE RECORD: "Please don't think I'd do all of that really and truly. Why, at heart I'm as meek as a lamb."

BACKGROUND

Alice was the last child born to Pierre Napoleon Berger, a grocery clerk, and his wife Marie Alphonse Foisy, both of French-Canadian ancestry. She had six siblings: Henry, Arthur, Eugene, Charles, Alfred, and Yvonne, a music teacher, who died of Bright's disease (nephritis) in 1896 at age eighteen. Alice was away at school and four months shy of fifteen when her father died. She adored Convent Villa Maria, a boarding school for girls of French and English heritage from the U.S. and Canada; "[t]he time I spent there was the happiest in my life," she said later. By 1905 she worked as an artist and lived at Henry's place in Manhattan, along with his wife, three children, Mom, and Alfred. In November, she married 32-year-old George K. Hollister, a farmer and "vineyardist" from Jerusalem, NY. It's uncertain when he first picked up a camera, but by 1909 he was a correspondent and photographer who covered the Boer War, the Spanish-American War, China, and Japan for the Museum of Natural History and other organizations. He joined Kalem later that same year.

George Kleine, Samuel Long, and Frank J. Marion (K-L-M) formed Kalem in 1907, and managed to lure the successful Sidney Olcott away from Biograph. In 1910 they became the first studio to ever shoot on-location outside the U.S. The "O'Kalem" unit made almost thirty films presenting realistic Irish characters, not the xenophobic "cartoonish drunkards" common at the time. In addition, they also filmed in England, Egypt, and Germany. Fractured over money disputes, Kalem joined Famous Players-Lasky, then was absorbed by Vitagraph. Olcott wrote for Famous Players-Lasky after it became Paramount.

Among Kalem's stock were Robert Vignola, actor/director who later directed for Poverty Row; Marguerite Courtot, "Kalem's top female attraction" from 1915-1927, star of *The Adventures of Marguerite*, a series often double-billed with the Helen Holmes serial *The Hazards Of Helen*; Alice Joyce, Kalem's most popular actress (1913), star of her own film series, and wife to fellow Kalem actor Tom Moore before leaving for Vitagraph in 1917; Harry F. Millarde, Alice's frequent costar of over forty films before leaving for Fox and marrying Fox actress June Caprice; and especially Gene Gauntier, first "Kalem Girl" and the "preeminent figure" at Kalem from 1907-1912, who wrote, acted, and co-directed a number of films while also headlining her own series, *Nan The Confederate Spy*.

Home in 1911 was Crotona Park East in the Bronx until Kalem sent their "camera operator" to the new studio in Jacksonville, Florida. Alice and their two children, Doris Ethel (1906-1990) and George Jr (1908-1976) tagged along, and the studio enticed her to appear in a moving picture or two.

MOVING PICTURES: SCHOOLS OF IMMORALITY

By A Woman's Wit (1911): Alice's first film was a "pleasing" Civil War drama of a Union soldier captured spying behind Confederate lines and the Southern girl who helps him escape, featuring J.J. Clark and J.P. McGowan.

The Colleen Bawn (1911): A great example of the "O'Kalems." Gene Gauntier, J.P. McGowan, Alice, and Sidney Olcott star in the famous Irish play by Boucicault, based on a true story: Cregan (McGowan) secretly marries Elly O'Connor (Gauntier), but his mother wants him to marry rich cousin Anne (Hollister) so their mortgage will be raised. Will Danny Mann (Olcott) commit murder to ensure the plan? "[A]lert, resourceful, and progressive ... the Kalem players may well be proud of their achievement." Shot completely on location in Ireland; Hollister was cameraman.

*From the Manger to the Cross; or, Jesus of Nazareth (*1913) portrayed the life of Jesus Christ from birth to crucifixion. One of the greatest undertakings of early cinema, it was filmed completely on-location with dozens of extras and took eight months to produce. The cast: R. Henderson Bland as Jesus, Gene Gauntier as Mary, Alice Hollister as Mary Magdalene (possibly the first to portray her on screen), and Robert Vignola as Judas Iscariot. Fritzi Kramer, of the outstanding blog *Movies Silently*, notes Gene Gauntier wrote the treatment – it was her decision to omit the Resurrection narrative – and may have co-directed alongside Sidney Olcott. Cinematography was by George Hollister, as part of the "El Kalem" unit.

Shooting was far from heavenly. Olcott and Hollister were attacked by an angry mob, released only after "much use of the sign language" and Olcott brandishing a revolver. In Jerusalem, gangsters demanded money in exchange for filming "privileges." After Olcott got the authorities involved, the gangsters threatened to mix in with the extras and retaliate.

Kalem wisely left; this is the main reason the "triumphal entry into Jerusalem" is absent from the film. Gene Gauntier later recounted how she and Alice Hollister were "almost crushed" by throngs of people celebrating the ritual of the Holy Fire during Holy Week.

The film premiered in late 1912 in a special clergy-only screening at Wanamaker's in New York, then to the public in 1913. Contemporary critics and audiences adored it. "It is not a *Passion Play*," gushed *Moving Picture World*, "[i]t is indeed a cinematographic gospel . . . beautifully conceived and full of a sweet and pathetic naturalness . . . remarkable." To modern eyes it is pretty "stagy," almost a collection of religious tableaux. "Essentially we are watching an animated gospel," writes Fritzi Kramer. "[T]here is a remoteness that the film never quite overcomes." She also points out that despite its overwhelming success – the film cost approximately $35,000 to make and grossed nearly $1 million – Kalem "refused to pay or credit Olcott or Gauntier accordingly." After Vitagraph took over Kalem, they reissued an edited version in 1919; this is the version that survives today. It was also reissued with narration and a musical score in 1938. The National Film Registry added it to their collection in 1998.

The Vampire (1913): Alice, "dressed in close-fitting silver silk," laid claim to the title of first screen vampire. Harold (Harry F. Millarde) loves Helen (Marguerite Courtot) but is lured from her by "adventuress" Sybil (Hollister). She drains his bank account and gets him fired, then leaves him. Harry, despondent and seriously considering robbery in order to get Sybil back, happens on a music hall presenting – surprise! – French and Eis doing their famous "Vampire Dance." Recognizing his own imminent destruction, Harry takes the hint and rushes back to Helen. "[H]uman and convincing . . . healthy and amendable and it seems likely to please widely."

The Lotus Woman (1916): Another vamp role for Alice. This time she's Juana, innocent South American girl who morphs into a siren after her beau Lopez (John E. Mackin) brings her to the rebel camp. Jilted Jerry Mandeville (Harry F. Millarde) joins the cause and Juana attempts (and fails) to seduce him; she succeeds with Everett, the man Jerry's girl Dagmar (Faye Cusack) married instead of him. Lopez and Everett both die in the revolution, a chastened Dagmar returns to Jerry, and Juana – left without anyone to control – commits suicide. Alice was billed as "the original vampire of the photoplay" in ads for this film, and critics liked her "consistent, admirable" portrayal: "[A] vampire who depends upon her mental appeal to entice her victims is a novelty." This is the last of her Kalems: She resigned in July 1916, following George Sr. the year before.

Milestones (Goldwyn, 1920) featured Alice, Lewis Stone, and Mary Alden in a saga of the lives and loves of a shipbuilding family over fifty years (1860-1910). Reviews were mixed. Some praised the historical accuracy and novelty of the concept, while others' interest in the repetitive situations hovered "close to zero." It was Alice's return to the screen after an absence of almost two years due to "illness" – not sure if her own or someone else's.

The Forgotten Law (Metro, 1923): Victor (Jack Mulhall), angry at his wife Margaret's (Cleo Ridgely) charge of infidelity, amends his will to give custody of his daughter Muriel (Muriel Dana) to his brother Richard (Milton Sills). Victor is shot, Margaret is implicated, and Richard gets Muriel. Later, when the real murderer – Rosalie (Hollister), a jilted lover of Victor's – confesses on her deathbed, a sympathetic Richard marries Margaret so they can be a family. If, like critics, you find this "highly exaggerated and unlifelike," get this: the gravely ill Rosalie confessed to her nurse. *Who happened to be Margaret!* Yeah. One can't help but wonder how Alice felt playing Rosalie; her character suffered from Bright's Disease, the same illness that killed Yvonne.

Married Flirts (M-G-M, 1924): Alice plays the small role of "Mrs. Callender" (no pies) in this "bright and entertaining" flick about dueling vamps. Nellie (Pauline Frederick) neglects her husband for her writing career; Jill (Mae Busch) vamps him away. Later, after becoming a famous novelist, Nellie vamps Jill's new man, teaching her a lesson before reuniting with her husband. Nellie is clearly inspired by Elinor Glyn – she throws a star-studded mah-jongg party featuring M-G-M luminaries John Gilbert, Mae Murray, Norma Shearer, and Aileen Pringle as guests.

The Dancers (Fox, 1925): A melodrama about "the wildness of the young generation" and its ensuing consequences, starring George O'Brien, Alma Rubens, and Madge Bellamy. Tony (O'Brien) goes to South America and buys a dancehall. Dancer Maxine (Rubens) loves Tony but he only has eyes for Una (Bellamy) back home, who has already forgotten him in a haze of parties and fast living. (Alice plays stepmother to this "victim of the jazz craze.") Tony finds out he is heir to a fortune and rushes home to London and his sweetheart; Una waits until the night before the wedding to admit an "indiscretion." Tony forgives her but the girl, pregnant and shattered, commits suicide. Tony returns to South America and starts life over with Maxine. Alice plays the peripheral Mrs. Mayne in her last screen appearance.

OTHER SORDID DETAILS

She was a classy vamp, this Alice Hollister. She didn't slink around in velvet. "I like to make my vampires psychological studies," she told *Film Fun*. "[S]uggest the lure rather than boldly employ cigarettes and divans and voluptuous draperies." She was warm, friendly, a "hospitable soul" who enjoyed entertaining. "Smiling comes naturally to me at home," she said. "Playing movie vampire roles is a self-delivered [sic] sermon." Movie magazines, as with the other vamps, made efforts to normalize her. "Guess how I spend several hours a week when I get through work too late . . . before dinner?" she allegedly told *Photoplay*. "[W]ith my little fishing rod, I catch the nicest little fish you ever ate!"

Alice lamented her status as "one of the few players" who never tread the boards. "I'd like most of all to have one season on the regular stage in some strong, emotional play," she told interviewer Pearl Gaddis. "I feel some stage experience is absolutely necessary to help me round out my picture work." Most agreed she was terrific even without it, using words like "glamorous," "brilliant," and "captivat[ing]" to describe her work. "After eight years she remains popular with movie fans," praised a 1921 article, attributing it to her dependence "on merit alone to win favor."

She and George Sr. hopped around Los Angeles, moving from Hollywood Blvd. (same block as actor Stanhope Wheatcroft, Thanhouser director William Howell, and House Peters Inc. director Walter De Courey) to Romaine Street in the Beverly Hills section, then Glendale. George Jr. appeared in 13 films, most notably as the baby Jesus in *From the Manger to the Cross*, then became a photographer like his father. Doris Ethel was in seven films, including *From the Manger to the Cross*, and was "Little Eva" in Kalem's version of *Uncle Tom's Cabin* (1913). She married cartoonist Walter Lantz in 1930.

George Sr. worked for Thanhouser from late 1915 to early 1917, and later with old friend Sidney Olcott at Metro. He was listed in the 1940 census as an "inventor," and he was passionate about it, inventing several contraptions for the movie camera, including a focus/enlargement device and "anti-static apparatus." He also worked on early three-strip color processing, but didn't care for it: "I hardly think that motion pictures in color, by any process, will be a success . . . the public would soon tire of them." His tricked-out camera was legendary in the business, and his pride and joy: "[he] thinks more of his camera than [he] do[es] of me," Alice once told a reporter. George Sr. died in 1952.

CASE CLOSED

Alice Hollister died in Costa Mesa, CA, on February 24, 1973, after several years suffering from dementia and vision loss. She was cremated and interred with George Sr. in the Great Mausoleum at Forest Lawn Memorial Park, Glendale, CA. Alice was 87.

MUGSHOTS

Alice in 1916. Photo courtesy the Media History Digital Library.

A scene from The Lotus Woman *(1916). Photo courtesy the Media History Digital Library.*

Alice in Milestones *(1920). Photo courtesy Terry Ann Smith.*

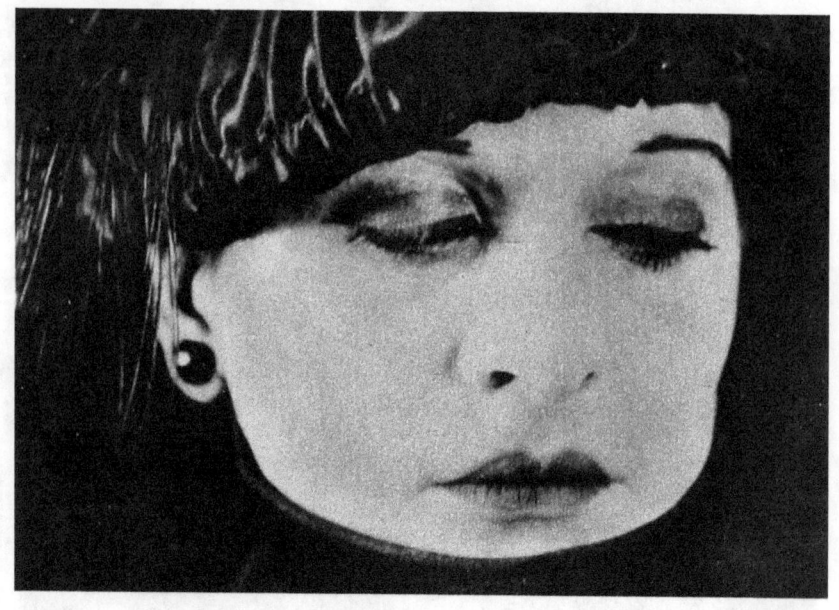
Photo courtesy Media History Digital Library.

FILE #31352: CARMEN PHILLIPS

REAL NAME: Anna Catherine Phillips
DOB: September 15, 1888 - Oakland, CA
HAIR: black
EYES: dark brown
WANTED FOR: reckless conduct
ON THE RECORD: "[A]s far as being afraid, I haven't the slightest bit of fear."

BACKGROUND

Anna was the last of four children born to "prominent resident" Manuel Phillips and Maria Freitas, three months pregnant when Manuel died suddenly at age 41. Maria, who wrote and spoke only Portuguese, struggled to raise her children while also caring for her elderly mother. By 1900, all the children were gainfully employed – Mary, the oldest, was a dressmaker, Joseph and Frank an ironworks heater and barber respectively – except for "Annie," who attended school through the eighth grade. In 1908 she made her debut as an "operatic contralto" in vaudeville, and joined the Princess Stock Company a year later. Her beauty, "splendid" voice, and graceful dancing in *The Sultan of Sulu* and *Piff, Paff, Pouf* (both 1909) made her an audience favorite. She became a principal for the Ferris Hartman Opera Company in December 1909.

What's more attractive than a songbird? Nothing, especially if she's a Florodora Girl. In February 1910 Annie was voted the most charming one in Los Angeles, which she attributed to plumage (changing her feathers nightly) and a balanced disposition: "frisky and cheerful, but you have to work in a little dignity." Her solos that July as "The Girl with the Eyes" in the Bristol Pier summer concert series necessitated extending the shows through the end of September. It was around this time that the *Los Angeles Times* noted "[s]he will one day be known upon the opera stage as a Bizet 'Carmen.' She fits the role so naturally..." The name stuck. Things also improved for the rest of the Phillips family: her siblings were married, Joseph was now a police officer, and both Mom and Grandma Freitas could read, write, and speak English.

MOVING PICTURES: SCHOOLS OF IMMORALITY

Carmen's first role was in *A Deaf Burglar* (Mutual, 1913). She appeared in several Keystone shorts that year, many featuring her old Princess colleague Fred Mace. She left in 1914 and freelanced over the next couple of years in films like *The Pipes of Pan* (Rex, 1914) with Lon Chaney and Pauline Bush, *Smouldering* [sic] *Fires* (Victor, 1915) starring J. Warren Kerrigan, Lee Moran comedies for Nestor, and Vitagraph shorts. What follows are Carmen's significant roles after her breakout year of 1916, and several serials from 1915-1925 in which she appeared.

The Yellow Girl (Vitagraph, 1916): Carmen starred as a dancer in this visually innovative "novelty" picture. Sets were closed to visitors and players carefully locked costumes away from prying eyes after shooting scenes. Edgar Keller, the film's author/director, artist, designed the sets while his wife, actress Nell Clark Keller, designed the costumes; the plot was later written around them. The plot itself was slight: Black (Webster Campbell), a painter, loves Flora, the florist (Florence Vidor in one of her first roles); and White (Alva Blake), his friend, loves Corrine the milliner (Corrine Griffith). Both men are "entranced" by the dancing of the Yellow Girl, Mlle. de Jaune (Phillips). Both women become jealous when Connie catches her posing for Black. The Yellow Girl confesses she commissioned him to do it, the two men reaffirm their love for their sweethearts, and all ends well. The high-contrast black and white photography was like a living Aubrey Beardsley sketch; critics called it "excellent" and "high-class."

The Cloud-Puncher, *Chased into Love*, and *There's Many a Fool* (all 1917) were Fox film comedies starring Hank Mann and directed by Charles Parrott, *a.k.a.* Charley Chase. The last of these was a "burlesque" on Theda Bara's incendiary *A Fool There Was* (1916), released on a double-bill with Bara's latest, *The Tiger Woman* (1917).

Forbidden Paths (Famous Players-Lasky/Paramount, 1917): Sato (Sessue Hayakawa) is in love with his ward Milly (Vivian Martin) but she loves Harry (Tom Forman). Harry adores Milly but gets roped into marriage by adventuress Benita Ramirez (Phillips). Sato, thinking only of his ward's happiness, lures Benita onto a boat and sinks it, opening the way for Harry and Milly's marriage. *Motion Picture* had kind words for everyone but Carmen, whose "makeup was terrible and her effort to be emotional worse."

The Cabaret Girl (Universal, 1918) was a Ruth Clifford-Ashton Dearholt drama where Carmen's bit role as Dolly was pivotal: She introduces the two leads, cabaret singer Ann (Clifford) and Ted (Dearholt), who proposes marriage despite his mother's misgivings. She convinces Ann of the poor match, and persuades her to "vamp" it up to drive Ted away. Ted discovers the ruse in time to save Ann from the lewd cabaret owner and all ends happily in this "well-acted" film with a "worn theme."

Whitewashed Walls (Exhibitors Mutual, 1919) is a "burlesque on Latin-American politics" – the whitewashed wall is where the dictator executes his enemies – starring William Desmond as Larry, an American who gets in trouble with the Mexican government and is saved by the dictator's niece Concha (Fritzi Brunette). Carmen is the mischievous Rosa, who satirizes "the well-known film vamp inimitably and looks the part."

The Home Town Girl (Famous Players-Lasky/Paramount, 1919) was a convoluted comedy/drama about John (Ralph Graves), country boy who makes good in New York, only to lose it all to a "city slicker." His small-town sweetheart Nell (Vivian Martin) tracks him down and sets everything right in the last reel. Some thought Carmen "overact[ed]" Nan, the tough, gum-chewing stenographer whose letter from John helps Nell find him; others found her "realistic."

The Pagan God (Exhibitors Mutual, 1919): The tagline: "An Oriental Adventuress Vamping an American Secret Diplomat." (Three guesses who the adventuress was.) Bruce Winthrop (H.B. Warner) is a secret government operative sent to stop Tai Chen (Phillips) and her Chinese rebellion. His fiancée Beryl (Marguerite de la Motte) is hurt by his attentiveness to Chen and calls off their wedding. Winthrop accepts both Chen's job offer and her confession of love, enabling him to steal the secret list of revolutionaries – but it falls into the hands of Beryl and her father, endangering their lives. Winthrop rescues them, Tai Chen kills herself, and Winthrop and Beryl wed. "Heavy and tragic" but thrilling enough to draw crowds; Carmen "in one of her best roles."

For A Woman's Honor (Exhibitors Mutual, 1919): Carmen has a good role amidst a formidable cast. Mannering (H.B. Warner), a captain in the British India Medical Corps, comes home to England to marry Helen (Marguerite de la Motte). Upon his arrival, Valeska (Phillips) insists she bore a child by Helen's recently-deceased father. Mannering pays her off to save the family pain; Helen and her mother witness this, think Mannering was involved in something indelicate with Valeska, and break off the engagement. Mannering returns to India and throws himself into his work. One day Helen, her mother, and Valeska – now friends – travel to India to visit Helen's brother Dick (John Gilbert), a customs officer accused of taking bribes from a renegade. Valeska attempts to seduce both Dick and the renegade, who shoots her and forces Dick to claim it was suicide. After illness and tribulation, the truth is revealed and Helen and Mannering are reunited. Despite the talent and picturesque setting, *Motion Picture News* thought it ideal only for those who liked "slow-moving dramas."

The Great Air Robbery, a.k.a. *Cassidy of the Air Lanes* (Universal, 1919) takes place in the future – 1925! Ostensibly about "air highwaymen" vs. the U.S. Postal Service, gold, and saving someone's *croix de guerre*, it's really a showcase for the brilliant stuntwork of Lieutenant Ormer Locklear. Carmen, Francelia Billington, and Allan Forrest made up the supporting cast. Locklear, the renowned "sky daredevil," got great notices for his work despite plot silliness. *Film Daily* noted with amusement the highwaymen's planes bearing death's heads: "It doesn't seem logical that pirates would advertise their profession so openly." *The Great Air Robbery* was released eight months before Locklear's death, his only film before the doomed *The Skywayman*.

Mrs. Temple's Telegram (Famous Players-Lasky/Paramount, 1920): Simple premise equals hilarity: Mrs. Temple (Wanda Hawley) decides to test the fidelity of Mr. Temple (Bryant Washburn) by locking him in a room with vamp Pauline (Phillips) all night. Hubby insists nothing happened; wifey pretends to disbelieve him, so he invents a tale about friend John Brown. Mrs. T. wires John Brown to visit and confirm the story – but it's the wrong John Brown, and he has a jealous wife of his own in tow. "The surprise finish is about the best thing," said *Film Daily*. "Highly amusing."

All Souls' Eve (Realart/Paramount, 1920): "Mild but pleasant" romance starring Mary Miles Minter in a dual role. Olivia (Phillips) is in love with Roger (Jack Holt), and arranges the murder of his wife Alice (Minter). Tortured by grief, he hires Nora (also Mary Miles Minter) as nursemaid to his son. Nora's belief in spirits combined with her tender love for the child convince Roger that Alice has indeed returned to the little family, and he marries her. Carmen's role existed solely to set events into motion, but *Film Daily* felt the vamping angle "improbable" and unnecessary.

The Heart Specialist (Realart/Paramount, 1922): Mary Miles Minter is Rosalie, a "Miss Lonelyhearts" columnist. Her editor wants to scratch it, but Rosalie sets out to find the true romance it lacks. She starts in a small Connecticut town where she's mistaken for the long-lost heir of Bob (Allan Forrest), a wounded war hero. She also discovers the hero's doctor (Noah Beery) and his sister, Grace (Phillips), are plotting to kill their patient before he discovers they've embezzled his estate. Once they realize Rosalie knows, they throw her down a well and Grace claims she's the real heir. Rosalie escapes, saves Bob from poisoning, Dr. Fitch is killed by toxic fumes in his laboratory, Grace is arrested, and Rosalie quits to become Bob's companion. The studio hired 35 wounded WWI vets as extras for the "interesting" film, a rare non-"sweet 16" role for Minter released a month after the William Desmond Taylor murder.

Thirty Days (Famous Players-Lasky/Paramount, 1923): John Floyd (Wallace Reid in his final role) must escape the fury of Giacomo Polenta (Herschel Mayall) after he mistakes Floyd's friendliness to Carlotta Polenta (Phillips) for flirtation. Floyd's solution? Punch a cop and get locked up. Only one problem: his new cellmate is Giacomo Polenta. Thanks to the intervention of the warden (Kalla Pasha) they both survive intact; upon release, the Polentas return to Italy, Floyd explains the mess to his understanding fiancée Lucille (Wanda Hawley), all's well that ends well. Critics singled out Carmen for her "keen sense of comedy" but felt that Reid was "entitled to a lot better stuff." He died while the film was in theaters.

Hollywood (Famous Players-Lasky/Paramount, 1923): This "Merton of the Movies"-style film starred two unknowns: Hope Drown and Luke Cosgrave, but is infinitely more famous for its 70+ cameos including everyone from Roscoe "Fatty" Arbuckle to Lois Wilson (and Carmen too). [Note: it was an early appearance for "Queen of the Hollywood Extras" Bess Flowers.]

Fair Week (Famous Players-Lasky/Paramount, 1924): Slim Swasey (Walter Hiers) is good at multitasking: he is guardian to Tinkle (Mary Jane Irving) while almost singlehandedly running the small town of Rome, Missouri. He loves banker's daughter Ollie (Constance Wilson), but when the fair comes to town, she falls for "Sure Thing" Sherman (Earl Metcalfe), the "fighting evangelist." Sherman is a crook working with Madame LeGrande (Phillips) to rob the town's bank; her job is to distract everyone with her hot-air balloon act. Tinkle climbs in the balloon basket, and overhears not only the plan, but the surprising news that LeGrande is her mother. She somehow alerts Slim who stops the runaway balloon, captures the crooks, recovers the money and wins Ollie's heart. The movie languished in the vaults for a while before release, and according to reviews – "faintly amusing," "distinctly inferior cast" – should've stayed there.

A Six Shootin' Romance (Universal, 1926) was a typical oater where the hero (Jack Hoxie) rescues the girl (Olive Hasbrouck) from the clutches of an evil rancher (William Steele). Carmen played the small role of the rancher's wife, her last screen performance.

Serials in which Carmen appeared included three for Universal: *The New Adventures of Terence O'Rourke* (1915), three complete two-reel adventure stories starring J. Warren Kerrigan as the title character and Phillips as Princess Constantine; *Lord John's Journal* (1915), a William Garwood five-episode mystery featuring Phillips as Jenny; and *The Great Circus Mystery* (1925), fifteen chapters of action/adventure with strongman Joe Bonomo, Louise Lorraine, and Phillips as Natchi. She also had a small role as Mimi in the King Baggot vehicle *The Hawk's Trail* (W.H. Productions, 1919), a fifteen-episode crime drama costarring Grace Darmond. Her best-known serial, and the only one that survives intact today, was *The Hope Diamond Mystery* (State Rights, 1921), starring Grace Darmond and inspired by true events surrounding Lord Francis Hope and "the most sinister jewel in history." Phillips had the dual role of Wanda Atherton in the British episodes and Miza in the Indian ones; Hindu servant Dakar (Britain)/Priest of Kama-Sita (India) was played by Boris Karloff. Story credit went to May Yohe, the former Lady Francis Hope.

OTHER SORDID DETAILS

"Two big brown eyes and a bewitching smile . . . brilliant and finely educated." With a resumé like that, Carmen had no shortage of admirers. One enamored (and plastered) gent imagined her onstage flirtatiousness was directed solely at him and was wounded by her "chilly indifference" backstage. Two hours after getting the bum's rush cops arrested him trying to break into her dressing room. The broker, despite being "well on in life," could not make the $12 bail and spent six days in jail. As the son-in-law of a local judge, retribution at home was probably worse.

As early as 1910-1911 she made headlines for speeding (68 mph!) – as a passenger, of course – in a "racing roadster" at the Motordrome and desiring to become the first "sky-chauffeuse" in America. "I'm just dippy about an aeroplane," she told the *Los Angeles Times*. "I'm sure I could learn to run one very easily, for I have always had a fondness for machinery." According to the article she also kept an album of plane pictures, a library of "aeronautic works," and could tell you the difference between a Curtiss, a Wright, or a Bleriot in detail. (This may be more than just puffery: in 1914 she was one of the first passengers on Walter Brookins' flight service from his hangar in Griffith Park.)

Mrs. Phillips was bedridden by 1915 and narrowly escaped burning to death after vengeful "tramps" to whom she had refused money, torched her house. Carmen shared her mother's luck: On Armistice Day 1918 she was riding in a car filled with merrymakers when it hit a telephone pole. Somehow, she, Mrs. Neely Edwards, and musical theatre actress Hazel Swanson escaped with only bruises.

Carmen married Swift & Co. salesman William Collier sometime after her mother's death in late 1924, and the two rented a place on Manning Avenue in Los Angeles. There was good money in wholesale meats and the Colliers lived comfortably until William's death in 1957.

CASE CLOSED

Carmen Phillips died in San Marino, CA of renal hemorrhage on December 14, 1966. She'd been suffering from multiple sclerosis for four years. Her friend Helen McGann reported her death; they'd met years before through their husbands at Swift & Co. Carmen was cremated, and her ashes interred at Live Oak Memorial Park. She was 78.

MUGSHOTS

Carmen in The Yellow Girl *(1916). Photo courtesy the Media History Digital Library.*

Carmen in 1916. Photo courtesy the Media History Digital Library.

Photo courtesy the Media History Digital Library.

FILE #42274: CLAIRE DE LOREZ

REAL NAME: Claire Deutch
DOB: August 4, 1895 – San Francisco, CA
HAIR: black
EYES: dark brown
WANTED FOR: international seduction
ON THE RECORD: "When it comes to the real technique of vamping... Claire shows 'em how it should be done"

BACKGROUND

Claire was the middle child born to cigar dealer Isaac "Ike" Deutch and Elizabeth McMahon. Pop was a colorful character, arrested in 1897 for running a slot machine at his cigar stand on Kearney Street. A year later he bought the "Crystal Palace" saloon at Kearney and Geary, making enough dough to buy their 1223 1/2 Geary Street house outright and hire a maid to help Elizabeth with Edward (1892-1932), Claire, and Thelma (1898-1980). Eddie and Claire danced at St. Brendan's for entertainment night, and the whole family was part of the social set, especially after Ike opened the "bar and merchants' lunch" on Market Street in 1905. Its dining room seated 100 and was "elegantly appointed" with paintings from the Crystal Palace; the ballroom was walnut with leather booths and electric lights. "Mr. Deutch starts business under particularly fortunate circumstances," said the *San Francisco Call*, "possessing great personal popularity and an establishment unusually favored in location and attractiveness." Somehow, both the Geary St. house and the café survived the San Francisco Quake (and resulting fire) seven months later, and Ike continued there until March of 1911, when he moved the lunch spot to 951 Market Street. The community protested, feeling a location devoted almost completely to "women's shops" inappropriate. He opened there anyway.

By 1915, Edward, liquor dealer and "young business man of San Francisco," wed Millicent Wood, stage performer and later Christy Poster Girl under the name "Millicent de Lorez." "Claire Dolores" played a featured role as "Woman" on the largest float in the same parade. Later that month, as members of the Paul Gershon School of Acting, she and Millicent performed in the annual San Francisco Press Club Show at the Orpheum. The theme was "Thirteen Years After," in honor of the

1906 quake/fire; the de Lorez ladies participated in "The Prohibition Minstrels," a tableaux mourning "Old Man Booze".

Peculiarities arose in the 1920 census. According to separate records, taken one day apart(!), Edward was a broker in stocks and bonds living with Millicent on Bush Street – but also a marine engineer living at the Geary St. home with Mom and Pop. Claire was a stenographer for an insurance company – but also an actress in "pictures" living on Witmer Street in Los Angeles. All corroborating info matches – these are definitely the same Deutches. Very strange. (The Witmer address is Claire's home in 1921 as well.)

MOVING PICTURES: SCHOOLS OF IMMORALITY

Father's Close Shave (Pathé, 1920) was Claire's first film, and maybe being uncredited was a good thing? Reviews were poor – "the laughs are certainly not too numerous" – for this second film in the "Jiggs"/*Bringing Up Father* series, starring Johnny Ray, Margaret Carrington, and Laura La Plante.

The Joyous Trouble-Makers (Fox, 1920): This romantic comedy starring William Farnum and Louise Lovely was the first of two films Claire made with Farnum (second was the detective picture *The Scuttlers* (1920), where she met friend Jackie Saunders). Average film, in which Claire played the small part of "Mrs. Denham."

The Four Horsemen of the Apocalypse (Metro, 1921) needs no introduction. Valentino smolders amid the rest of the cast, including Claire – billed as "Mlle. Dolorez" – as "Lucette, the artist's model." It wasn't much of a role, but just being involved in such a prestige picture increased her casting credit. "A masterpiece ... comes nearer the ideal than anything which has gone before."

The Queen of Sheba (Fox, 1921): One of *Educational Screen*'s "Fifteen Best Productions" of the year, with Claire finally in a prominent role! She played Queen Amrath, wife of Solomon, opposite Fritz Leiber (Caesar to Theda Bara's *Cleopatra* in the 1917 film) as the King and Betty Blythe as the Queen of Sheba. Years ahead of its time in making the film's climax a *female* chariot race between Blythe and Nell Craig as Princess Vashti; the race was supervised by Tom Mix and took 3500 workers, ten chariots, and thirty horses.

Claire suffered minor injuries that June while riding in a car with Thelma, musical comedy star Emlee Haddone, *Dramatic Mirror* Western manager Robert Doniel, and theater manager John Tenney. They were on a test drive from the Rolls Royce dealership when the car flipped on a rural road. Haddone suffered the worst of it and took eight months to recover.

Enemies of Women (Goldwyn, 1923): Another bit part in a film of exceptional quality. Lionel Barrymore and Alma Rubens star in the "powerful" Ibañez (*Four Horsemen*) romance; other uncredited actors include Margaret Dumont, Helen Lee Worthing, and Clara Bow as "girl dancing on table." Critics compared its lush atmosphere to a Stroheim picture, enhanced by location shots in Monte Carlo and Paris, and an epic sword fight.

Bright Lights of Broadway (Principal, 1923) was a drama of slimy producer (Lowell Sherman, of course) promising country girl (Doris Kenyon) stardom in order to, well, you know … while ex-protégé Connie (de Lorez) languishes, yesterday's news. Connie is killed in a struggle between the country girl's fiancé (Harrison Ford) and producer, and Tom is arrested for murder. It all works out in the end and Mr. Slimy Producer dies in a car crash. The film's plot was "conventional" but Claire got good notices for her "colorful acting."

The Net (Fox, 1923): Ridiculous melodrama starring Barbara Castleton and Raymond Bloomer. Don't believe me? Castleton's no-good husband kills her artist cousin, then pins it on an amnesiac (Alan Roscoe) who conveniently wanders into the studio. Eventually the husband is killed and the wronged wife and amnesiac fall in love and marry. Claire is "The Vamp," wherever that fit in. Amazingly, this received poor reviews. "Feeble attempt at entertainment," said *Film Daily*. "Terrible story."

Three Weeks (Goldwyn, 1924): Another bloated Glyn romance that did big business. Aileen Pringle is the Queen of Sardalia, fresh from leaving her debauched husband, who meets aristocrat Paul Verdayne (Conrad Nagel) and spends – you guessed it – three glorious weeks with him in Venice. Spoiler alert: Three years later the Queen sends for Paul, and though the king kills her in a jealous rage, Paul lives to see their "love child" crowned the new King of Sardalia. This is the film with the lounging on the tiger skin. Claire is "Mitze," the "gypsy companion of the king," and having this on her résumé earned her tons of publicity. Madame Glyn herself claimed Claire was "the most voluptuous woman in pictures" and, laurel of laurels, had "it"; of course, she also said Nagel had "it," so her judgment might've been a bit impaired. Generally good reviews, and some thought Claire would "arrest attention." An interesting aside: with its dark, foreign Queen and noble, Nordic Verdayne, the scandalous 1907 novel (and subsequent film) was not subtle in promoting the eugenics theory. As Bram Dijkstra says in *Evil Sisters*: "Glyn's implication was quite clear: if the colonized people of the world only act as wisely as [the Queen] and allow themselves to be 'mastered' into pregnant submission, the 'white man's burden' could be lightened immeasurably."

Beau Brummel (Warner Bros., 1924): Claire again has a small role as "Lady Manly," but look at this production! After the love of his life, Lady Margery (Mary Astor), marries another man, Brummel (John Barrymore) leaves the British army for a decadent dandy's life. He befriends the Prince of Wales (Willard Louis) and becomes the toast of Europe. Eventually, his extravagance with money and women, including the very married Lady Stanhope (Carmel Myers), get him run out of England to die alone in France. A success for Warner Bros, for whom it was a box-office smash – "absorbingly interesting ... one of the finest performances of [Barrymore's] screen career" – and for Barrymore and Astor, whose affair ended the moment he glimpsed Dolores Costello.

The Siren of Seville (Producers, 1924): Claire proved to be "a find" as "Ardita" in this Spanish bullfighting story "much on the order of *Blood and Sand*." Claire's "vamp" role is pivotal, as she distracts one matador to death and, later, she seduces the heroine's childhood sweetheart. The picture's reviews were mixed, some thought it "a corking picture" while others complained it was "too cluttered."

Her Night of Romance (First National, 1924): Claire's role of "returning actress" was unimportant, but look at with whom she was associating: Constance Talmadge, Ronald Colman, and Jean Hersholt in a "meandering little farce" of mistaken identity, where an heiress masquerades as a scrubwoman, a penniless nobleman as a doctor, and both wade through a series of complications before the truth comes out and they reunite for love. Kudos to *Educational Screen* for using the term "optience" for those in the seats. (Hey, they're not hearing anything, so ...)

With few exceptions, it was bit parts after this: *So This is Marriage* (Metro-Goldwyn 1924), with Lew Cody giving Biblical lectures; *The Range Terror* (FBO, 1925), where she "stands around clad in black lace and smokes and smokes"; *My Wife and I* (Warner Bros., 1925), a musty vamp story where Constance Bennett, not Claire, was the *femme fatale*; the crime drama *Under the Rouge* (Associated, 1925), with Claire singled out for notice as a "colorful cabaret vamp"; and the Canadian melodrama *The Northern Code* (Lumas, 1925). *The Re-Creation of Brian Kent* (Principal Pictures, 1925), based on the popular 1919 Harold Bell Wright novel of love, crime, and self-reinvention, listed Claire along with stars Kenneth Harlan, Zasu Pitts, Helene Chadwick, and Rosemary Theby, but her scenes may have been cut as she is absent from the official release credits. Claire also joined Reginald Denny and Julianne Johnston for the comedy-drama *Captain Fearless* (Universal, 1925), where a tough Confederate ancestor guides "a gallant young Southerner who hasn't the instinct to fight his battles in modern life." It appeared in several ads and articles from 1923 on, but was never released.

The exceptions were different indeed: *The Coast Patrol* (Bud Barsky Corp, 1925) was clearly no A-list blockbuster, but it provided Claire with a starring role as Valerie Toske who, along with Eric Marmont (Gino Corrado), runs a smuggling ring. Marmont tries to rope retired Naval officer John Slocum (Spottiswoode Aitken) and his ward, Beth (Fay Wray in her first major film role) into their disreputable plans, but Coast Patrol agent Dale Ripley (Kenneth MacDonald) is on to them. After a chance meeting, where Ripley saves Toske from drowning, she flips and helps him foil the plot and capture Marmont, who promptly commits suicide by jumping overboard. "[H]as a good production and a good story . . . competently cast and well- acted."

Cobra (Paramount, 1925) was more notable for Valentino and Nita Naldi than Claire's role as "Rosa Minardi." Plot was essentially Valentino "trying to fight down his weakness for women," and he looked marvelous doing it. Audiences enjoyed the film but cackled at the teary closeups of Our Hero "intended to excite sympathy." Best said about the rest of the cast was that it was "ordinarily adequate."

Claire traveled to France, returning to San Francisco in November 1925; soon after, she went again, returning to New York in March of 1926 – and promptly left for England, back in New York by August 1926. What prompted the constant travel? Boredom, exasperation, hunger for opportunity, all of which France promised in spades. She made the romance *Le soleil de minuit* (Films Legrand, 1926) as "Un amie" alongside Richard Garrick and Gina Manés (of Abel Gance's *Napoleon* a year later), France's "vamp with emerald eyes." It did the trick and, with her next project *Morgane la sirene* already in pre-planning, she left Hollywood "for good" in April 1927.

"For good" is a lot shorter than it used to be, and Claire was back by mid-June; word was, she'd return to France in July, finish her contract with Leonce Perret, "Europe's ace director," and then come home permanently to Hollywood. Paramount acquired *Morgane* for Europe but didn't release it until 1928, and the New York premiere was delayed even further to June 1929. Rex Ingram Studios in Nice was the shooting locale, and Perret – already famous for *Madame Sans-Gene* (1925) with Gloria Swanson – the artistic director. As with the Swanson film, production was under Franco Films, an ambitious international effort to distribute French films with "internationally known players" in the United States. Offices were established April 1929 in New York City, and the Craig Theater hosted the inaugural offering of *Morgane, the Enchantress* plus a color short of Mistinguett. The romantic drama starred Claire as the titular character, with support by Ivan Petrovich and Josyane. It's essentially a waterlogged vamp picture, with George (Petrovich), in love with Annette (Josyane), falling under the spell of the reclusive Princess Morgane de Bangor (de Lorez), a mysterious woman living in a castle and thought a mermaid by local fishermen (she dons a shiny swimsuit and long blonde wig during her daily swim. "[B]eautiful ... smashing bits of photography" gushed *Variety* over the castle's luxurious interior shots and the exteriors by the Brittany seaside. Unfortunately, they didn't stop there: "[The] story is hopeless. It wouldn't qualify in America as second class magazine fiction. Titling is terrible, stilted, and provoking laughs." Other critics agreed. Mordaunt Hall, over at the *New York Times*, noted "[W]hen the Siren of Aval Castle, in Brittany, made her bow it aroused unintended merriment ... not only due to the subtitles, but also to the acting of Claire de Lorez." *Photoplay* wasn't kind, either: "[O]ne of the worst to reach our shores. The direction and technique are of 1915 vintage and the acting is ham *de luxe*." *Hollywood Filmograph* thought it "entertaining throughout" and Petrovich "ably supported" by Claire, but audience opinion sided with the former reviews. The delay even rendered costumes, the last resort during an awful picture, passé. It closed in a week. Franco Films' "virtually washed up," managed one more film (the non-Claire *Figaro*), then closed by November.

Claire returned to Paris at the end of January 1928. Germany and France entered into an agreement in the late 1920s to bolster their respective film industries; UFA had "recovered from financial collapse," and for France – "in a state of constant crisis with regard to its finances and its production processes" – a partnership was especially lucrative. International actors were cast to increase appeal to the European market, and Germany provided funding (and occasionally facilities). *L'Equipage* ("The Crew") was distributed by the Alliance Cinematographique Europeéne, the Paris subsidiary of UFA, and may have been made in Berlin; director Maurice Tourneur spent time there in August 1928. Succinctly described by *Variety* as "the French 'Wings'," the plot involves two WWI aviators, played by Jean Dax and Georges Charlia (later in *Prix de Beauté* [1930] with Louise Brooks) in love with the same woman (de Lorez). *Variety* was not impressed. "Perhaps the last atrocity of the late lamented war ..." Continuity problems were patched with "long-winded" and "sappy" intertitles; Claire vacillated between "dead pan" and "mugging."

Claire's final film role was a small one: "Suzy Gloria" in *La venenosa*. Released in France in October 1928, it starred superstar singer Raquel Miller as Miss Liana, a circus acrobat who brings the "kiss of death" to anyone who loves her. Though Miller had a following in the U.S., it's doubtful the film ever reached the American market.

OTHER SORDID DETAILS

During December 1923, Claire met Dr. Montrose Bernstein, a Detroit physician vacationing in Hollywood. The two fell in love and he stayed in Hollywood, investing his money in oil and real estate. By June of 1924, he and Claire were engaged, with the wedding "to occur shortly after the doctor returns from the East." Claire planned to remain an actress, and traveled to Portland in September for *The Greatest Thing* (*Under the Rouge*'s working title) when suddenly, on September 28, she was transported back to L.A. "on the verge of death as a result of a serious intestinal complication." She allegedly fell ill while lunching with Jackie Saunders, who noticed her friend's "nervousness". Thelma had Claire admitted to California Hospital, where she underwent surgery Oct 5. Her condition remained "very grave."

Reminiscent of the 1920 census, there's another version: She was stricken with severe "appendicitis" while readying to leave for Portland. "It's all for the best," said Claire. "I wouldn't be here to say it if it had happened on the train." One thing missing from both accounts: Bernstein. There's nothing about him until June 1925, when the gossip columns report "Claire De Lorez's [sic] solitaire is gone – by intent... seems she had a lot of quarrels with [Bernstein], and everything is all off." Bernstein remained in Hollywood, married, and became a well-known physician, featured in society pages well into the 1960s.

Wondering what the other Deutch siblings were up to? Thelma danced in *Earl Carrol's Vanities of 1923* and toured with the show in 1924; by 1929 she danced at a Cairo nightclub, billed as formerly with the "*Folies Bergère de Paris*." Eddie, possibly separated from Millicent, joined the Merchant Marine around 1922; ten years later, he died of a heart attack while at sea. Claire returned to California and Geary Street in April 1929, and how much time she spent there is hazy. Perhaps she met up with Thelma, who came to California in the summer of 1930 to study "off-rhythm" and tap at the Bud Murray School before touring Europe again. Things were uneventful until September 1932.

"ACTRESS TAKES LETHAL POISON – DEATH WITHIN WEEK FORECAST BY PHYSICIANS"

On the night of September 24, at a bustling Paris café, Claire downed a bottle of bichloride of mercury tablets after her fiancé, "socially and politically distinguished" Evangelos Typaldos-Bassia of Greece, suddenly refused to marry her after living together for a year. His parents did not approve of the romance, begun in 1926, and ordered him back to Athens immediately to assume an "official position" in their shipping company – and an arranged marriage. An observant waiter refused Claire water and followed her to the bathroom so she couldn't swallow; a doctor who happened to be there by chance induced vomiting. Both saved her life. Thelma, Claire's bulldog in tow, immediately rushed to her sister's side. Claire recovered enough to return to the U.S. in January 1933, where she lived for six months in what the media called a "trial separation from a Greek prince." Her "confidant," Dr. Bernstein, had his own suspicions about her suicide attempt: "[she] had beauty, wealth and fame, but they could not compensate for lost love."

Her life became a quiet, private one. A 1934 article chronicled her career, noting Madame Glyn's "sufficient guarantee" of eternal stardom. She returned to France during the 1940s, serving as secretary of the Paris Post No.1 American Legion Auxiliary. Her name resurfaced in Walter Winchell's column in June of 1944, but for a very different reason than motion pictures: The "silent film pet" was held at Vittel, a former French resort in which the Nazis housed British and American expats. Jewish detainees were sent to Auschwitz. Living conditions still resembled the resort, with hotels, a large park, classes and lectures, even a tennis court and theater. Residents had heat and hot water, received visitors, and did their own cooking; however, they were still prisoners and barred from leaving the grounds. The Nazis conveniently left this – and the large, barbed wire fence surrounding the camp – out of promotional materials boasting Vittel the example of standards at all their camps. Vittel was liberated three months after Winchell's article, in September 1944. Five years later Claire Typaldos-Bassia (so they married after all!) was accosted by three men outside her home. They leapt from a car, demanded her purse, and stripped her of $25,000 worth of jewelry.

Despite her terrible experiences overseas, she frequently traveled between France, England, and Geary St. in San Francisco during the early to mid-1950s. In 1957 her address changed to the Plaza Hotel in New York City, and by 1959-1960, it was 2088 Golden Gate Avenue, Thelma's home. Thelma lived there until her death in 1980.

CASE CLOSED

Claire de Lorez's death information remains unknown. Several places erroneously list September 21, 1985, which is for another Claire with a different birth date and mother's maiden name. I believe her passing to be at least before Thelma's, since her obituary listed no survivors.

MUGSHOTS

A boyish Claire. Photo courtesy the Media History Digital Library.

Claire in 1924. Photo courtesy the Media History Digital Library.

Claire in Morgane, the Enchantress *(1929). Photo courtesy the Media History Digital Library.*

Photo courtesy the Media History Digital Library.

FILE #73579: DE SACIA MOOERS

REAL NAME: Franc'Anna (or Franc'Annie) Saville
DOB: November 19, 1888 - Port Huron, MI
HAIR: blonde
EYES: "fiery brown"
WANTED FOR: sedition against brunettes
ON THE RECORD: "This is no job for the silly little fluttering moth nor the philandering salamander ... [t]hey don't belong to the vamp corps at all."

BACKGROUND

Franc'Anna, renamed "De Sacia" by age two, was the first child born to civil engineer Frank Saville and Victoria Crandall. They'd actually moved to California shortly after their 1885 marriage; De Sacia's younger sisters Ruby (1890-1941) and Ruth (1892-1985) were born there. The three girls, the only children out of eight to survive, went to St. Gertrude's Convent School. De Sacia continued on to the fancy prep institute Marlborough School, but it's unclear if her sisters did.

The headstrong De Sacia eloped in 1906 with Edwin Demarest Mooers, "heir to the millions made by his father in the Yellow Aster [gold] mine." She was 21, he was 49. Mooers, a dilettante and "spendthrift millionaire," moonlighted as a chorus boy in New York for a while and had previously eloped with his first wife. In 1908 their son Douglas was born. De Sacia, Ruth, and Ruby all worked as "chorus girls" in opera; by 1910 the Mooers, along with Edwin's mother, lived in Los Angeles while the rest of the Saville clan remained in San Francisco. All except for Ruth, that is: the seventeen-year-old met Robert "R.J." Connors, a well-known "traveling salesman" twelve years her senior, while visiting cousins in Portland OR. Her cousins were supposedly taking her to Europe for vocal training when "Count Von Meyer" took a liking to her; R.J. told him to knock it off, and the Count challenged him to a duel, which wasn't necessary. Frank and Victoria, who'd arranged the Oregon/Europe trip to keep Ruth away from Connors, learned of the marriage via telegram.

De Sacia's first stage notices were for *Dark Rosaleen* (1919) at the Majestic, "a new Irish comedy of today." Cast included Charles Bickford and Thomas Mitchell. By 1920, she was the unofficial queen of the "younger 'millionaire set' of Southern California," a featured member of the Morosco stock company, and played bits in Dolores Cassinelli's *The Virutous Model* (1919) and films with Montagu Love and Theda Bara. Hearst Newspapers additionally crowned her "America's Most Beautiful Blonde." De Sacia was bubbly, ambitious, and opinionated. Take vamps, for instance. Onscreen, she complained, they always had "coal-black hair" and "scintillating black eyes," yet the opposite flourished in her high-hat clique's nightclubs and house parties.

"[A] blonde is the greatest of all vampires," she insisted. "No brunette who ever lived . . . can lure and trap a man so quickly." She agreed to act under her maiden name for a year in order to prove her theory. "I don't want any money," she said. "I've plenty of money of my own." Her first project? Vitagraph's film version of her own 1920 book, called (what else?) *The Blonde Vampire*. Dedicated to her friend, novelist (and perhaps ghostwriter?) Eleanor Browne, it followed the antics of Marcia Saville, heir to the Golden Poppy Mine, who "inherited a capacity for both decency and mischief." De Sacia's manager, Allen Rock, organized the publicity blitz: book reprints, a song tie-in, a portrait by Henry Clive. She already had "favorable recognition" from several producers, and everyone expected *The Blonde Vampire* to be a "screen spectacle." Vitagraph, however, felt the opposite strongly enough to shelve it. Rock sued for possession in late 1921, arguing De Sacia's $100,000 worth of costumes would be unfashionable if they waited any longer. Vitagraph won the suit, claiming no partnership with either party other than proper payment. Wray Physioc, *Blonde*'s director, took over production, and finally saw release through FBO in April 1922 as part of Wid Gunning's value-priced "Entertainment Series." A girl's gotta eat while waiting for her official debut, however . . .

MOVING PICTURES: SCHOOLS OF IMMORALITY

The Mystery Mind (Educational, 1920): De Sacia had a small part in this fifteen-chapter serial headlined by J.R. Pauline, "the world's greatest mesmerist," Violet MacMillian, and villain Paul Panzer in his last major serial role. The adventure story, "the first psychic serial," concerned an heiress (MacMillian) marked for death by a gang led by "The Wolf" (Panzer) and the disembodied voice of "The Mystery Mind." Will her fiancé (Pauline) save her in time? To whom does the diabolical voice belong? Earned a favorable enough response to garner Pauline, long time roadshow and vaudeville star, a long-term contract as detective "Oliver Optix" opposite Dorothy Mackaill in a series of dramedy shorts. (They were never made.)

Son of Tarzan (National Film Corp. of America, 1921) was another small role for De Sacia in what several critics and fans call the most faithful adaptation of one of Edgar Rice Burroughs' books, and the first Tarzan story made into a serial. P. Dempsey Tabler was Tarzan, Kamuela Searle his son Korak, Karla Schramm was Jane, and Nita, Martan Meriem. The popular fifteen-chapter serial was later edited into the feature film *Jungle Trail of the Son of Tarzan* (1923) by Burroughs himself.

The Blonde Vampire (Wray Physioc Inc., 1922): *Motion Picture News* thought De Sacia's acting "commendable," the film "conservative and appealing." The plot, built around woman's alleged "caveman instinct" [i.e. women desire dominant men], involved notorious flirt Marcia choosing tough guy Tom "The Snapper" Smith (Alfred Barrett) over loyal but dull Martin Kent (Edwin August). The other gangsters suggest Tom marry Marcia for her money, but he refuses, sparking an underworld battle. After Tom's former moll saves his life, he returns to her – and Marcia to Martin, realizing excitement isn't worth the trouble.

The Challenge (American Releasing, 1922): Small role of Peggy Royce opposite Dolores Cassinelli, Rod La Rocque, and Warner Richmond in a "thoroughly enjoyable" love triangle drama set amongst the Adirondacks.

Potash and Perlmutter (First National, 1923): The two leads, Barney Bernard and Alexander Carr, reprised the roles they originated in the smash Broadway hit. Abe Potash (Bernard) and Morris Perlmutter (Carr) are living the dream as partners in a bustling clothing store – until someone in the shop is murdered during a workers' strike and their bookkeeper, Irma Potash's (Hope Sutherland) sweetheart Boris Andrieff (Ben Lyon), is framed. The two men work every angle to prove Andrieff's innocence, including helping him flee to Canada (which gets Abe Potash in hot water). Eventually the real murderer confesses and all ends well. The comedy-drama blend, the first release from Samuel Goldwyn's independent production company, was called "very human . . . one of the best of the season," with an "excellent cast," including Vera Gordon as Mrs. Rosie Potash and Martha Mansfield as the head model. De Sacia's role as designer Ruth Goldman wasn't central to the plot, but it introduced her character type: "business vamp." Business vamps, she argued, should be in every executive's arsenal. She is alluring, engaging, a kind of "woiking goil" / golddigger hybrid with a stylish car and chic flat "where she gives entertainments for the clients of her employer." She is also, of course, beautiful – and preferably blonde. "Blonds [sic] are the best bets as business vamps because they are more subtly appealing than brunettes. No one ever knows quite what new schemes are being hatched . . . ." As for inviting businessmen into one's home, well, "[t]here is no moral issue involved with the business vamp's life . . . for the woman of wit and charm this career is one to conjure with."

For brevity's sake, since the majority of her sixteen other roles were bits, only the prominent ones follow.

The Average Woman (State Rights, 1924): "Flaming youth" Sally (Pauline Garon) is in love with reporter Jimmy Munroe (Harrison Ford), but being courted by "society chap" Rudolph Van Allen (David Powell). Van Allen, threatening to blackmail her judge father with letters concerning her dead mother, lures the flapper to the roadhouse he secretly owns; suddenly the place is raided and Sally's good name "compromised." The girl is, of course, exonerated, and Van Allen killed by jealous former lover Mrs. La Rose (Mooers), clearing the way for Sally and Munroe's romance. Not the most original plot, but director Christy Cabanne credited with lending intelligibility to the whole tangled mess. "Well above the average picture ... clever work [from] a carefully selected and distinguished cast."

Forbidden Waters (Metropolitan Pictures-Producers Dist. Corp., 1926) was "[a]ll about a sweet young thing who got a divorce but didn't really want it." Nancy (Priscilla Dean), newly parted from husband J. Austin Bell (Walter McGrail), burns rubber out of Reno and lands in a California jail on speeding charges. Her love rekindled thanks to his rescue (and bail), she spends the rest of the film keeping vamp Ruby (Mooers) and her partner-in-crime Sylvester (Casson Ferguson) away from him. (She doesn't know Bell, still in love with his wife, is encouraging Ruby on purpose!) Nancy "shanghais" him to an island with a waiting preacher. Ruby and Sylvester are arrested. The End. "[I]nteresting even though the story is slight ... Casson Ferguson and De Sacia Mooers a clever but unsuccessful pair of crooks."

Broadway Nights (First National, 1927): A romantic drama with a dash of *A Star is Born* (1937). Dancer Fannie (Lois Wilson) gains fame through the help of famous MC Johnny Fay (Sam Hardy). [Note last name.] They marry, have a child, and team up for an act. Two producers catch it and offer Broadway to Fannie – but nothing to Johnny. She turns it down, ruining them professionally while Johnny's compulsive gambling ruins them personally. Fannie gets work in a musical comedy, but it flops until she suggests they hire her husband. He saves the show and they save their marriage. *Broadway Nights'* snappy titles were by Jack Conway, editor/writer for *Variety* who coined slang like "bimbo," "palooka," and "scram." The nightclub sequence, featuring De Sacia as real-life Queen of the Speakeasies Texas Guinan, is remarkable for three young "showgirls" making their movie debut: Sylvia Sydney, June Collyer, and interestingly, Barbara Stanwyck.

De Sacia played Guinan-esque roles twice more, as "Tex" in *By Whose Hand?* (Columbia, 1927) and Rene, a bleached-blonde "'whoopee' cabaret owner" in *Just Off Broadway* (Chesterfield, 1929). The latter, a silent underworld drama with Ann Christy and Donald Keith, disgusted *Photoplay*: "[The characters] make bally whoopee, drink wood alcohol, and blow one another's brains out. Pass it."

The Arizona Kid (Fox, 1930): De Sacia's last movie was a bit part in this sequel to *In Old Arizona* (1929). Warner Baxter was the "World's Most Loveable Bandit" (the Cisco Kid renamed to avoid copyright lawsuits). The Western also featured Mona Maris and Carol (no "E" yet) Lombard. It did well, though "not as well knit as its predecessor."

OTHER SORDID DETAILS

So, who were the better vamps, blondes or brunettes? *Movie Weekly* ran a contest the summer of 1922 to find out. Entrants provided four photos (fancy dress, figure, closeup, closeup profile) and a short essay on "The Art of Luring – Why I Know How." To help contestants, the magazine offered special advice columns each week by celebrity vamps: Betty Blythe for the brunettes, De Sacia for the blondes. [Note: redheads were lumped in with blondes.] The winners received either a contract with Pyramid Pictures or a role in Ed Wynn's new stage show. "It may mean a big opportunity for you." Copious photos of the two peppered with Ziegfeld girls illustrated each column, where they advised recruits to study "sex lure" closely. "Have you ever noticed the way a baby looks at you, or the way a baby kisses? That is precisely the way this girl parts her lips and ensnares the man." (No comment.)

De Sacia didn't worry about her reputation, but her manager did. He carefully seeded newspapers with non-vamp publicity like "kindness classes" taught in the summer of 1923 for New York City schoolchildren, complete with photo of De Sacia tenderly accepting a kitten from an adorable moppet. Another well-worn tactic: she can't help it, she's French, the article rife with *cheries*. She and Mooers divorced, "in order that she could continue her picture career," and she and Rock tied the knot in June 1925, but with the end of acting came the end with Rock. Their union was officially annulled in December 1929, Rock stating De Sacia's first marriage "was not properly terminated," but they'd been separated since at least 1926. She wed current beau Harry L. Lewis as soon as legally able. Lewis was an amalgam of her previous husbands: gold prospector, oil speculator, sports correspondent for the *San Francisco Bulletin*, publisher of weekly sports magazine *The Referee*, boxing promoter, horse racing manager, and race track developer. (Wonder if he had any hobbies?) De Sacia found "contentment" as a homemaker, kept up with Hollywood through the

Film Welfare League, and served as director for the McKinley Home for Boys. She and Lewis remained happily married until her death.

Ruth's marriage ended by 1920 and she moved back in with Mom and Dad, Victor in tow. She acted a bit in the teens, mostly Broncho Billy pictures at Essanay, and continued acting on stage through the 1930s. She even did a little TV work in the 1950s and 1960s. Ruby married in 1925, moved to San Francisco, and became Bon-Ton's celebrated "corsetiere" through the 1930s. She died at age 51 of a cerebral hemorrhage.

CASE CLOSED

De Sacia Mooers died in Los Angeles following a short illness on January 11, 1960. Her obituary mistook her for Dorothy Dwan, calling her Tom Mix's leading lady in *The Great K & A Train Robbery* (Fox, 1926); no mention of vampires, blonde or otherwise. She was 72.

MUGSHOTS

Slightly scary De Sacia. Photo courtesy the Media History Digital Library.

Vanity. Photo courtesy the Media History Digital Library.

De Sacia in The Blonde Vampire *(1922). Photo courtesy the Media History Digital Library.*

Photo courtesy Newspapers.com.

FILE #28096: EDNA TICHENOR

REAL NAME: Edna Frances Tichenor
DOB: April 1, 1901 - St. Paul, MN
HAIR: black
EYES: brown
WANTED FOR: loitering, but sinister
ON THE RECORD: nothing other than her "inscrutable Slavik [sic] mold of face"

BACKGROUND

Edna was the second and only surviving child born to Ira Tichenor, a newspaper man, and Hattie Craig. The family moved to Los Angeles in 1904, and by 1910 Ira was comfortably supporting the family as a real estate editor. Edna attended Long Beach Polytechnic High School and married high school sweetheart Robert Joaquin Springer in January 1918. Two years later, they took in Hattie while Ira was away editing a financial column for a paper in Salt Lake City, UT. Robert, an auto mechanic, supported them.

MOVING PICTURES: SCHOOLS OF IMMORALITY

How Edna got into movies is hazy, though she appeared to have some experience as a dancer. She is first mentioned in a *Motion Picture* article about new faces in film, alongside Barbara La Marr and "Ramon Samanyagos" (Ramón Novarro). Nearly all her roles were bits or uncredited, so info will be included on all of them:

Drifting (Universal, 1923) was Edna's first film and the start of a fortuitous pairing with Tod Browning. Cassie Cook (Priscilla Dean) is smuggling opium in China with Jules Repin (Wallace Beery). When Jarvis (Matt Moore), a mining engineer, takes a little too much interest in their doings, they decide to kill him. Cassie discovers he is an undercover agent, and as she is secretly trying to get her addict friend Molly (Tichenor) away from the menace, they collude to bring down the entire operation headed by evil Dr. Li (William Mong) and his daughter Rose (Anna May Wong). Of course, they also fall in love. Reviews of the melodrama were mixed, some finding it dull, others describing it as exciting with "effective acting."

The Gold Diggers (Warner Bros., 1923) had a small role for Edna as "Dolly Baxter" in the first film adaptation of the Broadway smash. Uncle Stephen (Wyndham Standing) objects to his nephew's (John Harron) engagement to chorus girl Violet Dayne (Anne Cornwall), since they are all golddiggers. Violet's friend, Jerry La Mar (Hope Hampton), decides to "super-vamp" Uncle Stephen so that Jerry looks tame by comparison, and he takes the bait, giving the young couple consent. Only problem is, now Jerry's in love with Uncle Stephen! The story transferred well to film, with critics praising the "clever and subtle" comedy for never losing its "sparkle." Remade in 1929 as *Gold Diggers of Broadway*, and adapted as *Gold Diggers of 1933*.

Maytime (Preferred Pictures, 1923) is famous among modern audiences for a). being an early Clara Bow role and b). the popular 1937 Nelson Eddy-Jeannette MacDonald remake. The plot was simple: kids from the wrong side of the tracks (Harrison Ford, Ethel Shannon) were forced apart; years later, their grandchildren fall in love and marry, achieving the happiness earlier generations could not. Edna was originally cast as a society lady, a role that instead went to Bess True. Modern cast lists include Edna as "Cleo," but she was uncredited at the time of release and does not feature in any publicity. (Interesting aside: two children in the film were played by Jacqueline Wells, who would become 1940s starlet Julie Bishop, and Madison [Pat] Wing, frequent bit actress and sister to the "most famous chorus girl in the world" Toby Wing.)

One Night in Rome (Metro-Goldwyn, 1924): Another tiny role for Edna as "Italian maid" in this drama of secret identities, star-crossed lovers, and revenge amongst noblemen starring Laurette Taylor and Tom Moore. Adapted from the stage play of the same name by J. Hartley Manners, its author and Taylor's husband. "Lavishly produced" but bland society drama. [Note: some newspapers and trade magazines claim Edna was the "vamp" in Harold Lloyd's *Girl Shy* (1924); contemporary reviews list only leads, and modern reviews name Nola Luxford.]

The Silent Accuser (Metro-Goldwyn, 1924): This fellow Peter seems to be the whole show: Peter the Great (a German Shepard akin to Strongheart and Rin Tin Tin) is the only witness to the murder of Barbara Jane's (Eleanor Boardman) stepdad. Jack (Raymond McKee) follows the dog back to the scene and is promptly arrested for the crime. Peter the Great helps him escape from jail and the three run off to Mexico, where the dog tracks down and forces a confession from the real murderer. Edna, again, has a bit role as "The Painted Lady." Peter the Great was a "remarkably well-trained, intelligent animal" poised for stardom when, on June 6, 1926, he was shot in the neck during a drunken dispute between his trainer, Ed Faust, and dog breeder Fred Cyriacks. He died June 18.

The Merry Widow (Metro-Goldwyn, 1925): There's so much already written about this film and von Stroheim's erotic decadence that I'll keep it brief: Brothers (John Gilbert, Roy D'Arcy), both princes, fall for the same American showgirl (Mae Murray). "Complications and misunderstandings" ensue, along with ballroom dancing and blindfolded musicians. (How's that for a synopsis?) Amidst the laundry list of peripheral (and uncredited) characters is Edna as "Dopey Marie." The romance was a "leader among program leaders" and still considered one of the era's most sumptuous films.

The Gosh-Darn Mortgage (Pathé, 1926), a Mack Sennett parody of "the old-time drama involving the mortgage on the old homestead" starring Thelma Parr, Charles Farrell, Peggy O'Neil, and Edna as (shock!) "The Vamp." The comedy short got good notices – "lively and funny all the way ... all [the cast] do their share to make this number worth while [sic]."

Officer of the Day (Fox, 1926): A man joins the U.S. Navy to ask a consul for his daughter's hand, then struggles with switched luggage, rival suitors, and a "burlesque chase climax." Harold Goodwin, Eugenia Gilbert, and Brooks Benedict starred, and Edna was again "The Vamp." "Lively comedy," said *Motion Picture News* of the comedy short. "[S]naps into high speed right at the start and maintains its breezy action to the finish." Edna made only three more pictures, all for Metro-Goldwyn-Mayer, but oh, what pictures they were:

The Show (1927), Edna's second collaboration with Tod Browning, was lurid, weird, and wonderful. (Can you tell I liked this?) Cock Robin (John Gilbert), a miscreant carnival barker, falls in love with "good girl" Salome (Renée Adorée). The Greek (Lionel Barrymore), the show's snake-oil salesman, is also infatuated with Salome and tries to eliminate his competition. Salome hides Cock Robin, who is softened by her compassionate heart, and their path to happiness clears after the venomous lizard The Greek intended for Cock Robin bites and kills him instead. Edna is memorable as one of the "sideshow freaks," a human-spider hybrid named Arachnida. The image of her head atop a giant web is one of the most indelible of the era. The plot wasn't unique – *Film Daily* called it yet another "hero-villain-girl affair" – but Browning's phantasmagorical imagination and clever direction elevated it to "arguably the closest approximation of *Caligari*'s expressionism that Hollywood had yet attempted."

London After Midnight (1927): Browning's original story, titled "The Hypnotist," explored the theory that a criminal placed under hypnosis can be made to repeat their crime. Volumes exist on this "Holy Grail" film, so, again, brevity: Roger Balfour (Claude King) is found dead of apparent suicide, a cause that doesn't sit right with his executor Hamlin (Henry B. Walthall). Five years later, the now-abandoned Balfour estate has new renters: the macabre-looking Man in the Beaver Hat (Lon Chaney) and his assistant Luna (Tichenor). The spooky new neighbors prompt Hamlin, living next door with his nephew Arthur (Conrad Nagel) and Balfour's daughter Lucile (Marceline Day) to investigate. Eerie goings-on at the mansion become a retelling of the night of Balfour's death, and suddenly a killer is revealed: Hamlin, who killed Balfour after he refused his request of Lucile's hand in marriage. The Man in the Beaver Hat is Inspector Burke of Scotland Yard, trained to use hypnosis to draw out the culprit of Balfour's "suicide." Other players were Percy Williams as the dead man's butler, and Polly Moran as Miss Smithson, assistant detective disguised as the new maid. Browning's story was heavily influenced by the stage production of Bram Stoker's "Dracula," and while Chaney's makeup was grotesque – pointed teeth, bulging eyes – it was Edna, with her diaphanous white gown and heavily kohled eyes, that exuded the "wraithlike" vampire vibe. It was the most profitable of the Chaney-Browning films, though reviews were mixed and many felt it didn't do Chaney's career any favors. It would also be Edna's last appearance on screen. The film was remade by Browning in 1935 as *Mark of the Vampire*, with Carol Borland assuming the role of Luna.

West of Zanzibar (1928), released with a synchronized score and sound effects, is familiar territory. Phroso (Lon Chaney), a magician, loses his wife Anna (Jacqueline Gadson) and the use of his legs thanks to rival Crane (Lionel Barrymore). Anna returns only to bear an infant daughter before she dies. Eighteen years later, the three have relocated to Africa. Crane is a successful ivory merchant, Phroso a powerful tribal leader called "Dead Legs Flint," and Maizie (Mary Nolan) – Crane and Anna's infant daughter – a ruined child of the brothel and barroom due to Flint's vengeful "influence." Crane is killed in an attack by the natives, and their customs require Maizie to be sacrificed on her father's funeral pyre. Only then does the truth come out: she was Flint's child all along. Devastated, Flint offers the girl the only gift he has left: using his old stage trickery to take Maizie's place on the pyre, allowing the girl to escape. Commanding performances drew audiences, but they and critics were tiring of the "Browning-Chaney freak circus." They made just one more film together, *Where East Is East* (1929), before Chaney's untimely death in 1930. Edna's role as a dancer in the seedy Zanzibar Club was cut from the final print. *Zanzibar* was remade in 1932 as *Kongo*.

Edna's specialty dance number in *Susan Lenox: Her Fall and Rise* (1931) was scrapped, so her cinematic swan song was as stand-in for Dorothy Burgess in the Columbia voodoo horror-thriller *Black Moon* (1934), starring Burgess, Jack Holt, and Fay Wray.

OTHER SORDID DETAILS

Edna was divorced by 1930, living with Mom and Dad on Sunset Boulevard. Sometime before 1936, she took the name "Frances Duzan" and, returning to her dancing roots, worked as a showgirl in New York. Not sure where the name came from, since the only Frances Duzan in the 1940 census was born in 1914 and worked as a chemical engineer; nevertheless, it was under that name (and maiden name Tichenor) that she remarried in 1944. The groom, Henry West (1899-1980), was born Heinrich Oberlander in Czechoslovakia and became wardrobe/costume designer on more than twenty films including *The Charge of the Light Brigade* (Warner Bros., 1936), *Robot Monster* (Astor Pictures Corp.,1953), and *Heller in Pink Tights* (Paramount, 1960). He was working as an assistant director at the time of Edna's death.

CASE CLOSED

Edna Tichenor, one of the most mysterious and intriguing women in movie history, died at Cedars of Lebanon Hospital on November 19, 1965. Cause of death was "purulent peritonitis" from a perforated intestine due to post-operative adhesions following a hysterectomy. She was cremated at the Chapel of the Pines (Pierce Bros. Mortuary) and her ashes given to Mr. West. She was 64.

MUGSHOTS

Lovely Edna. Photo courtesy the Media History Digital Library.

Edna at her vampy best. Photo courtesy Newspapers.com.

Photo courtesy the Media History Digital Library.

FILE #62042: IVA SHEPARD

REAL NAME: Iva Blanche Shafer
DOB: April 23, 1886 – Cincinnati, OH
HAIR: black
EYES: blue/hazel
WANTED FOR: blackmail, pseudocide, general wantonness
ON THE RECORD: "Iva Shepard says any screen kiss lasting more than six feet of film is just a matter of business."

BACKGROUND

Iva was one of four children born to Nicholas and Candice ("Candas" on census), her siblings were older brother Clifford ("Cliffert" on census, born 1882), older sister Bessie (born 1884), and little sister Pearl (born 1891). Her early years were spent in Chicago IL, where Nicolas worked as an advertising agent. By 1906 she toured the Pacific Northwest with the Willard Company in *Hickory Farm*, showing "really great capabilities, especially as regards her emotional work." She and theatrical manager Perry Girton wed in Seattle WA in March 1908; she joined the Girton Stock Company as an "ingénue" in early 1909. After a short departure for Hollingsworth she rejoined Girton and his new Bentley Stock Theatre in L.A. as their leading woman, "one of the prettiest and most popular leading women we have yet had." (If her husband didn't write that copy, he should have!)

MOVING PICTURES: SCHOOLS OF IMMORALITY

Iva made a number of early films with Selig, the first being *The Wife of Marcius* (1910), a tale of ancient Rome written by and starring Hobart Bosworth. The others were outdoorsy dramas and Westerns, featuring Bosworth, Tom Santschi, and Eugene Besserer.

The Coquette (1911): Iva is Ida, "lame" sweetheart of fisherman Hugh (Santschi); after he saves Mabel (Betty Harte) from a shipwreck, she vamps him away, angering Ida's brother (Herbert Rawlinson). After the two men tussle – at one point tumbling off a cliff – Hugh realizes his error and things end happily (and predictably) for Ida. Unusual in that Iva is collateral damage, rather than perpetrator, of the seduction.

A Diplomat Interrupted (1912): Iva reverted to type as a daughter willing to offer her "virtue" to save her father from financial ruin. *Moving Picture World* was horrified by the drama's plot and argued it "outraged human probability, common sense and even decency." Selig and Iva parted ways in 1913. Afterwards, her films were for various studios (Rex, Powers Picture Plays, etc.) under the distribution umbrella of Universal. Here's a select few:

The Fight Against Evil (1913) was a white slavery "cautionary tale" starring Margarita Fisher as the innocent Mary Fisk; the hero of her eleventh-hour rescue, Dr. Lawson (director/producer/actor Robert Z. Leonard), devoted his life to protecting "girlhood flowers" (*ewww*) from vice and destruction. Not sure who Iva played in this; betting it was one of the "red-lipped songsters" occupying the villain's home.

In Slavery Days (1913): Here's a "fine convincing story of ante-bellum [sic] times," and by that, they mean nauseatingly racist: Mammy Sue (Shepard), the "octoroon," switches her baby with that of the planter and his wife, so that she might grow up wealthy and free. (I know you're wondering: Mr. Warren, the planter, was away on a *three-year* business trip; Mrs. Warren was blind. Even in 1913 they didn't buy it.) A grown Carlotta (Edna Maison), young mistress of the house yet Sue's real daughter, fumes over fiancé Robert Thornton's (Robert Z. Leonard) attraction to true Warren child Tennessee (Margarita Fisher). When things look serious, she forces Sue to spill the beans, stunning Thornton, then callously sells Tennessee onto a steamboat. Thornton chases after the steamer and Carlotta runs to her mother's cabin, where they quarrel; somehow it catches fire and they both burn to death. Thornton catches up just in time to save Tennessee from a lecherous slave buyer and they, of course, marry.

His Own Blood (1913): If you thought New Coke was bad .... (Man, I dated myself with that joke.) Dave Harding (Edwin August, also director) is making bank with his soft drink recipe. Frank, his drunkard son (Frank Hallack), is making time with "wild company." Harding dissuades the boy from his habit and returns him to fiancée Eileen (Ethel Davis). A grateful Frank decides to try Pop's pop, believing anything from his father must be "wholesome and good." He's quickly hooked by the "insidious drug" secretly included in Harding's formula and becomes ... a "fiend." A crushed Harding learns only an operation can save Frank from certain death. As he consents to the surgery, the "pure food authorities" investigate and ban production of the soft drink. Frank recovers and marries Eileen; Harding shutters his factory and donates all proceeds to charity. This warning about soft drinks – "one of the great evils" of society – got lukewarm reviews. "[W]ell-acted and generally pleasing," said *Moving*

Picture World, but the operation plot point was "ridiculous." Iva left Universal and freelanced after 1914.

The Straight Road (Famous Players/Paramount, 1914) was Clyde Fitch's popular play about Moll O'Hara (Gladys Hanson), dissipated tenement dweller, and her struggle against the sins of the "slums." Peppered with a prizefight subplot and colorful characters like Big Bill the saloon keeper (William Russell); the lascivious Douglas Aines (Arthur Hoops), who tries in vain to ruin Moll; and Lazy Liz (Shepard), who doles out "the untamed, the fearless and the furious jealousy characteristic of her environment." *Variety* thought it a "good story with a moral" that didn't lose humanity, and *Moving Picture World* commended the entire cast for their "strong scenes" of "straight dramatic quality."

The Hand That Rules the World (Universal, 1914): Another social drama written, directed, and starring Edwin August. Edwin (August) longs to settle down with wife Eva (Shepard) and start a family. Eva, "consumed with but two things, her dog and her gowns," sneers at motherhood and takes up with another man. Edwin and Eva divorce, and in the space of two years Eva bears a child to her lover while Edwin, happily remarried, rejoices in his children. (You see where this is going.) Outcast by her fair-weather friends, abandoned by her lover to the "sordid life" of an unwed mother, Eva's thoughts turn to Edwin. She finds his home, quietly peers in the window; met by the idyllic sight of Edwin playing with his family, Eva slinks away, overcome by "darkness and despair." The ending sounds bleak but no further info about it could be found. Maybe there wasn't any. *Moving Picture World* felt the plot needed "greater clearness and better effect."

The Drifter (Mutual, 1916): Compulsive gambler Harold Derwent (Alexander Gaden) is hardly a model divinity student, and after expulsion takes up at the track with adventuress companion Madge (Shepard). On board a train, his luck and money gone, he meets doppelganger Rev. William Ashton (also Gaden), heading for a new town and congregation. The train crashes, the pastor is killed and, sensing opportunity, Harold assumes his identity. Once things are settled, the pastor's wife joins him, and – shocking twist! – is the former Faith Willis (Lucile Taft), Harold's one-time sweetheart. After seeing his benevolence to his flock, she keeps the secret, but not so Madge, who blackmails Harold into playing the ponies on the church's dime. There is a terrible accident and "Rev. Ashton" is called to the jockey's bedside; the two instantly recognize each other, and the jockey confesses to hiding the money in a stall. Madge is furious and tries to expose Harold, but Faith defends the good reverend, and what better character witness than a pastor's wife? She and Harold, suddenly cured of gambling, travel to a distant city, quietly marry, and return to their quiet lives of ministry. "There is every reason to believe 'The Drifter' will be well received by audiences," said *Motography*. The story was "admirable," and the "enjoyable" racetrack scenes "add[ed] color to the picture." As for Iva, an acting manual's caption synopsizes her performance: "Cruelty. Evil. Vengeance. Malevolence. Venom. Vampire."

The Haunted Manor (Mutual, 1916): This "elaborately produced" Mutual Masterpicture Deluxe was associated with Iva for the rest of her life. She played Zoe Trevor, adventuress and favorite mistress of the Rajah (Henry W. Pemberton). When she falls for American artist Craig Pitcairn (Earl Schenck), the suspicious Rajah sends his henchman Singh (William H. Hopkins) to spy on the lovers; Zoe accidentally stabs him to death, prompting the Rajah to threaten retribution unless they wed. She flees to America, with Pitcairn close behind, and they marry. Tortured by her loving husband's ignorance of her past, Zoe decides her cousin Edith (Gertrude Robinson) would make a more suitable wife – and fakes her death to clear the way. Through the machinations of jealous model Celeste (Olive Trevor in her movie debut) and the manipulations of not-so-sweet Edith, Pitcairn lands at the business end of an angry mob prepared to lynch him for murder. Zoe appears at the last moment to clear his name, he insists her past means nothing to him, and they happily reunite. Oh, and the Rajah follows them to America, but refrains from vengeance after Zoe's faithful servant Khula (Robert Clugston) takes responsibility for Singh's death. Gaumont built an East Indian enclave in St. Petersburg Florida, decked Iva out in $6000 worth of jewels, and hired an "entire circus" to complete several scenes. A news blurb about Iva riding horseback in the circus parade admired her adventuresome personality: "She has always been used to doing just exactly what she wanted to do... [t]he charming actress is afraid of nothing." Trade papers attested to her vamping abilities: "Miss Iva Shepard, the Gaumont (Mutual) 'vampire,' used forty-five feet of celluloid ribbon to record a kiss upon the lips of Earl O. Schenck. Earl came up pale, but smiling." (The full movie was 5000 feet.) Despite the expense, the film disappointed critics who felt it not up to the usual Gaumont standard. "[T]he telling of the story shows carelessness... [but Iva] handles the part assigned to her capably."

The Street of Seven Stars (General Film Co., 1918): A glimpse into the lives of "an interesting collection of human beings," based on the story by Mary Roberts Rinehart (though moved from Vienna to Paris) and the first film produced under Doris Kenyon's DeLuxe Pictures Inc. Harmony Wells (Kenyon) is an American violin student, whom Dr. Byrne (Hugh Thompson) loves from afar. Harmony is too career-driven to notice, but after the death of a beloved patient, an invalid boy (Stephen

Carr) abandoned by his mother (Shepard) for the stage, she forsakes music to marry him. "Picturesque" and "pretty," particularly the mountain scenes, but "the too common mistake" of cramming in every detail of the novel resulted in "chaos." This was Iva Shepard's last film.

OTHER SORDID DETAILS

1916 was the height of Iva's "vamp" persona. Articles dotted newspaper and fan magazines, in addition to the aforementioned *Haunted Manor* publicity. Chira, palmistry's "ablest and best-known expert," proclaimed Iva's hands "as near a perfect type as can be found . . . ." As befitting a vamp, they were "more of the masculine type," conducive to shaping "her own destiny regardless of consequence." The *Cincinnati Enquirer* supported this: "All her life Iva Shepard has been successful in whatever she has undertaken." *Motion Picture* thought her "the only vampire who can successfully "vamp" with light blue eyes" (though the 1919 *Motion Picture Directory* calls them "hazel").

Iva, by then split from Girton, lived with Mom and Dad on Broadway in New York City. The Shafers moved to Manhattan after a brief 1910 stint with Pearl and her theater actor husband Charles Yorba in Los Angeles CA. The marriage barely lasted past the thank you notes, and Pearl was remarried to Charles Canfield by late 1912. Iva wed stage/movie actor Lyle Clement in 1918, and began touring again with stock companies, including the Wilkes Theatre of Salt Lake City, UT. She was named its leading lady by 1921 and a year later the actors (including Willard Mack) took over the closing theater, renaming themselves The Salt Lake Cooperative Players. Her hard, wisecracking Mabel "never missed a trick" at the Morosco's 1923 western premiere of *The Gold Diggers*, and by the late 1920s she was based in California, doing comedy.

Iva and Clement divorced by 1930 and Iva moved back in with Mom and Dad, this time in Venice, CA. She remained there through the 1940s and the death of her father. She continued stage acting, including *Life with Mother* (1952) with Leatrice Joy at the Pasadena Playhouse. Iva also did three TV shows in 1955: a small role on the Western TV anthology *Death Valley Days*, in "The Homeliest Man in Nevada" (S4E4), and two episodes of *I Love Lucy*.

"Don Juan and the Starlets" (S4E17) was the plum role. Ricky stays out late doing movie publicity; Lucy nods off on the sofa waiting for him. He comes home early the next morning and, rather than wake her, freshens up and heads to work. The maid (Shepard) arrives to find Lucy still asleep on the sofa, so she quietly straightens up after Ricky and slips out. When Lucy (finally!) awakens to a pristine house and unused bed, she assumes

Ricky partied with the young starlets and never came home. Lucky for him, the maid "'splains" and saves his neck.

"Nursery School" (S5E9) was a Little Ricky-centered episode. Lucy reluctantly obeys Ricky's wishes and sends Little Ricky to nursery school, where he promptly comes down with tonsillitis and must have them removed. Lucy, realizing Little Ricky is at the hospital without his favorite teddy bear, dresses as a nurse and conspires to sneak it to him. Iva and Maxine Semon play nurses.

She was retired by the 1960s and, according to great-niece Linda Bucci, "lived a quiet life with her sister." Iva and Pearl lived together in Los Angeles until Pearl's death on New Year's Eve, 1964. Ms. Bucci fondly remembers her great-aunt treating her to lunches at the Clifton Cafeteria in Pasadena, where she would tip everyone handsomely, "even gas station attendants."

CASE CLOSED

Iva Shepard died of pneumonia and complications of heart disease in Arcadia, CA on January 26, 1973. She was cremated and shares a niche with Pearl in the Mausoleum of the Golden West at Inglewood Park Cemetery, Los Angeles, CA. Iva was 86.

MUGSHOTS

Iva isn't pleased. Photo courtesy Linda Bucci.

Iva circa 1915. Photo courtesy the Media History Digital Library.

Iva in The Haunted Manor *(1916). Photo courtesy the Media History Digital Library.*

Photo courtesy the Media History Digital Library.

FILE #53537: MARCIA MANON

REAL NAME: Elizabeth Harrison
DOB: October 28. 1895 - Sacramento, CA
HAIR: dark brown
EYES: dark brown
WANTED FOR: assault and battery on The Girl with the Curls
ON THE RECORD: "I try so hard to make the part consistent that I even hate myself sometimes."

BACKGROUND

"[H]er real name is Camille Ankroiwich," wrote *Motion Picture* Magazine in 1918, born in Paris to Italian mother "Jane Ward of the legitimate stage, her real name being Camillia Gramini" and Russian father "Julien Ankroiwich, a musical director in the Palais D'Royal Theater, Paris." The article was titled "Marcia Manon – Film Sphinx" . . . and Theda Bara taught us that the Sphinx of the Fan Magazine's riddles are always applesauce.

She was the second child of Wallace Harrison, a painter, and California-raised Camille / Camellia Ward. Marcia's brother Julian was born a year earlier, and the family called Los Gatos, CA home until 1910, when they moved to Burbank. Dad became a "paint contractor," and they took in Camille's sister Violet, a nurse. Life was ordinary for Marcia; she attended school and performed in recitals at the First Methodist-Episcopal Church in Sacramento. In 1915, she married "auto livery" man Daniel Kathan; it was Kathan's second marriage, and was over by April 1917, about the time Marcia changed her name to Camille Ankewich and started in motion pictures.

MOVING PICTURES: SCHOOLS OF IMMORALITY

Marcia claimed her first role was an uncredited Apache dancer in the Lou Tellegen romantic drama *The Victory of Conscience* (1916). "Mr. Tellegen laid his hand upon my head for a second. I burst into tears . . . I was tired . . . [t]hey incorporated that into the scene."

The Prison Without Walls (Lasky, 1917): Helen Ainsworth (Myrtle Stedman) is interested in prison reform. Her fiancée and estate manager, Norman Morris (William Conklin), is secretly a crime boss and jealous of

Conroy, the reformed convict (Wallace Reid) whom Helen hired as her secretary. Morris bribes his mistress, their maid Felice (Marcia as Camille Ankewich), to plant stolen jewelry in Babbs' room – and orders his flunkies to murder him. Conroy overhears (and narrowly escapes) the plot, but Morris's Plan B is staging a burglary. Conroy is arrested, and Morris implicates Felice as an accomplice (why not clean up two messes at once?). He and Helen go to the governor, who is waiting for them. Surprise! Conroy, actually prison expert Huntington Babbs, already sent a letter explaining the ruse. Appearing from another room, Felice and Gilligan, the hired burglar and (unbeknownst to Morris) old friend of Conroy, confess the entire thing was Morris's idea. The cops hustle Morris away, but not quickly enough; Felice shoots and kills him. Helen, of course, ends up with Babbs. Wallace Reid always brought audiences in, but critics thought it only "fair program material." Marcia had a small role in another Reid vehicle, the war drama *The Hostage* (Lasky, 1917).

Stella Maris (Famous Players-Lasky, 1918): Marcia's immortal role, opposite dual Mary Pickfords as wealthy invalid Stella Maris and abused orphan Unity Blake. While Stella's loved ones, including her favorite, John Risca (Conway Tearle) build a fantasy world of princesses and knights to protect her, Louise, Risca's drunken tyrant of a wife (Marcia as Camille Ankewich), hires Unity as their maid, then is arrested for savagely beating the girl. John adopts Unity, who promptly falls in love with him. Meanwhile, thanks to an operation, Stella leaves the house for the first time and enters a world very different from her magical kingdom. The two girls meet, each a bright spot for the other, but Stella's heart sinks further after learning of John's wife. Unity, overwhelmed with compassion, performs a final act of gratitude and kills herself and Louise so that Stella and John can be together. Pickford's inspired performances of Stella and Unity drew raves from critics and audiences alike, but while reviews lauded the "very good work" of "remarkable character woman" Manon, the horrified public couldn't get past her pummeling America's Sweetheart. The studio anticipated this and prepared a snipe for local newspapers and theater programs:

"While Miss Camille Ankewich gives a splendid interpretation of the brutal woman, she is a woman of gentle disposition and dearly loves little Mary. Marshall Neilan, the director, said that he experienced the greatest difficulty in getting Miss Ankewich to beat Miss Pickford ... [she] burst into tears and declared it was the hardest thing she had ever done in her whole life." Marcia took pride in the result: "I don't suppose I shall ever do better work, for I put everything there was in me in that drunken, fighting tigress."

One More American (Famous Players-Lasky, 1918) was a heartfelt little drama about Luigi Riccardo (George Beban, quintessential portrayer of "the Italian in America"), living in Little Italy without his wife Maria (Marcia as Camille Ankewich) or daughter Tessa (Mae Giraci) for the last five years. They are on the way to America when, after Luigi refuses to pay a bribe, ward boss Regan threatens to bar his naturalization papers and have Ellis Island doctors declare Maria and Tessa unfit to enter. Reporter Sam Potts (Jack Holt) catches wind of the situation and arranges a phony bribe in exchange for Luigi's papers. Sam then exposes Regan, freeing Luigi to welcome Maria and Tessa with open arms. "Simple, direct, appealing and full of fine human touches," said *Motion Picture* Magazine, and *Moving Picture World* thought Camille Ankewich a "stand out" as Maria. Marcia's personal favorite of her films, and the last in which she used her old stage name.

Old Wives for New (Famous Players-Lasky, 1918): Marcia has the small role of "Viola" in this C.B. DeMille drama about Charles (Elliott Dexter) who, tired of his wife Sophy (Sylvia Ashton) after twenty years, takes up with Juliet (Florence Vidor); when a murder pushes them both into the spotlight, Charles and Juliet flee to Italy, each with decoys (Charles' is Viola) to throw off rumors. Back at home, Sophy gets a divorce and finds happiness with Charles' (male) secretary.

Savage Woman (Select, 1918): Marcia played the small supporting role of "Aimee," the jealous former lover of costar Milton Sills, in this adventure story of mistaken identity, kidnapping, and a heroine (Clara Kimball Young) who raised herself in the wilderness.

The Test of Honor (Paramount, 1919): Wealthy Martin Wingrave (John Barrymore) is having an illicit affair with Ruth Curtis (Manon). When her husband finds them, she blames Martin, and the two men fight. Afterwards Curtis, sick with a weak heart, needs his medication - which his wife purposely does not administer. Curtis dies and Wingrave is imprisoned for manslaughter. After seven years he returns to provide for his neighbor Juliet (Constance Binney) and exact revenge on all who have wronged him. The excitement over Barrymore's first screen drama sparked hyperbolic reviews: "it is so good a picture there seems to be a lack of words that might adequately voice its praise," cried *Variety*. "[A]bout as fine a piece of work as Mr. Barrymore has ever done...." They didn't leave out Marcia, either: "[t]here is a 'vamp' in the picture who looks like a comer ... the way that that woman can use her eyes...."

She made another film with Mary Pickford, *Captain Kidd Jr.* (Artcraft, 1919), a broad Keystone-esque farce that was one of Pickford's weaker offerings, then two films with Bessie Barriscale: *The Woman Michael*

Married (1919) and *Life's Twist* (1920). More vamp roles, like Associated Productions' *The Forbidden Thing* (1920), where her dance hall girl Glory Prada seduces James Kirkwood away from Helen Jerome Eddy (don't worry, they shot Glory later); Goldwyn's society comedy *All's Fair in Love* (1921), where Vera, the town vamp, forms a love triangle with May Collins and Richard Dix (critics really liked Marcia in this); and Paramount's convoluted society drama *Ladies Must Live* (1921), where John Gilbert, Leatrice Joy, hell – everyone in the film is in love with someone they can't have. Manon starred in crime dramas (*Skin Deep*, First National, 1922), more society dramas (*The Greater Glory*, First National, 1926), and copies of *The Big Parade* (*Heaven on Earth*, M-G-M, 1927). Also, how many vamps do you know who can claim an independent film about the Inuit on their résumé (*Justice of the Far North*, C.B.C., 1925)?

A welcome exception was the Frothingham-produced *The Woman He Loved* (American Releasing Corp., 1922) starring Manon and the drama's writer, William Mong, as refugee "Russian Jews" Nathan and Esther Levinsky. Once in the U.S. Esther despairs of their meager existence and runs off with Max Levy (Fred Malatesta), sending son David to foster with the Danvers family. Years later, Nathan owns a prosperous ranch that butts up against the Comstock ranch. Comstock (Charles French) despises Jewish people and has no idea that Jimmy Danvers (Eddie Sutherland), the boy his daughter Helen (Mary Wynn) is engaged to, is actually David Levinsky. Jimmy learns of his true parentage and goes looking for Nathan, newly reunited with Esther after a fire ruined his ranch (and a philandering Levy ruined Esther's relationship). Helen and Comstock follow Jimmy, and after Nathan rescues Helen from disgrace at the hands of Levy, a grateful Comstock gives the young lovers his blessing. Critics appreciated its message against discrimination, but the film only did tepid business.

Marcia's final film was a small role in 1929's *Love, Live and Laugh* for Fox, a melodrama starring George Jessel (in his first talking picture) about an Italian hurdy-gurdy man. There were trade paper rumors about playing a nurse in 1930's *All Quiet on the Western Front* but it appears it never came to fruition.

OTHER SORDID DETAILS

All of the puff pieces say her birth name was Camille Ankewich, and her movie name came from "Marcia Manot," Geraldine Farrar's character in Paramount's *The Devil-Stone* (1917). (Apropos, since some saw a likeness between the two actresses.) Syndicated notice of the change ran in mid-January 1918. She was fine with her new name, but felt "a little sorry" that she would never be known as Ankewich, *a la* Nazimova.

Publicists whipped her faux heritage into a fire-and-ice persona: "[A]ll my emotions are so intense that I am almost afraid to give them full reign," she reportedly told *Motion Picture Classic*. "Marcia Manon is as exotic as an orchid," wrote *Motion Picture* Magazine, "with the temperance of a diva, the beauty of an Egyptian princess, the languorous grace of a black panther."

The real Marcia was almost dull by comparison. "I live a very plebeian existence in Los Angeles with my mother and brother ... [w]e give little musical affairs on Sunday nights to our friends. That is about the limit of my social life." She enjoyed music and hoped to make a career of it, but "I reached nineteen, and still my ideas were far away. I decided to try doing extras in the movie studios." She dedicated herself to improving her craft: "[y]es, I like the screen, and I like the people, and I am perfectly content – so long as I am assured that I am making progress. You must work to succeed; work hard, unwaveringly ... [n]othing comes by chance." The result was becoming "one of the most popular of the Famous Players-Lasky actresses," voted eighth in *Motion Picture*'s "favorite vamp" write-in contest.

She and producer Joseph "J.L." Frothingham married at Mom's Beverly Hills home on September 27, 1919. The Harvard grad initially oversaw motion picture investments for E.H. Rollins & Sons, but soon switched to manager of Bessie Barriscale Studios and a member of The Associated Producers, a group of independent producers and directors akin to United Artists (members included King Vidor, Thomas Ince, and Mack Sennett). His sterling track record for signing and managing "rising young stars" featured Marguerite de la Motte, Barbara La Marr, and Helen Jerome Eddy among others. Marcia took a break after the wedding: "I was glad to rest," she said, "for I had been in the grind so many years." She spent her days reading, driving, and decorating their Cahuenga Avenue apartment (next door to J. Warren Kerrigan).

Julian rented a room about two miles away on Fountain Avenue. Already known for his "unusually striking" watercolors and sketches, he worked as art director on films like *Dante's Inferno* (Fox, 1924) and *The King of Kings* (Pathé, 1927). Another project was his face; he underwent plastic surgery on his nose and mouth in 1926.

Frothingham owned several show dogs and was an active fixture in the world of canine competition. On October 31, 1925, in San Diego's Balboa Park, he was judging the fourth annual Hollywood Kennel Club dog show when he suddenly crumpled, dead of a stroke at 45. Marcia moved to Burbank to live with her mother and brother; Wallace died in 1929. After Camille's death in 1937, the two siblings rented houses together on South Hobart Boulevard and Hammond Street. By the 1950s they were living apart, Julian still producing "compelling" artwork for local connoisseurs, Marcia still calling herself a motion picture actress (perhaps extra work?). Julian died in Los Angeles on October 20, 1965.

On November 12, 1969, Marcia was driving her pickup with friend Florence Hopper, 83. She stopped at a train crossing, then inexplicably "pulled into the path of a southbound Union Pacific train." The truck was struck on the right and both ladies ejected before it rolled down an embankment; Hopper was dragged 65 feet and pronounced dead at the scene. Marcia sustained only minor injuries. Her last years were marred by congestive heart failure and a small bowel obstruction that required a resection.

CASE CLOSED

Marcia Manon died of sepsis at Loma Linda University Medical Center in San Bernardino on April 12, 1973, the result of a pelvic abscess after her hysterectomy. She is buried at Inglewood Park Cemetery, Los Angeles, CA. Marcia was 76.

MUGSHOTS

Marcia in Stella Maris *(1918). Photo courtesy the Media History Digital Library.*

Marcia and John Barrymore in The Test of Honor *(1919). Photo courtesy the Media History Digital Library.*

Marcia in 1918. Photo courtesy the Media History Digital Library.

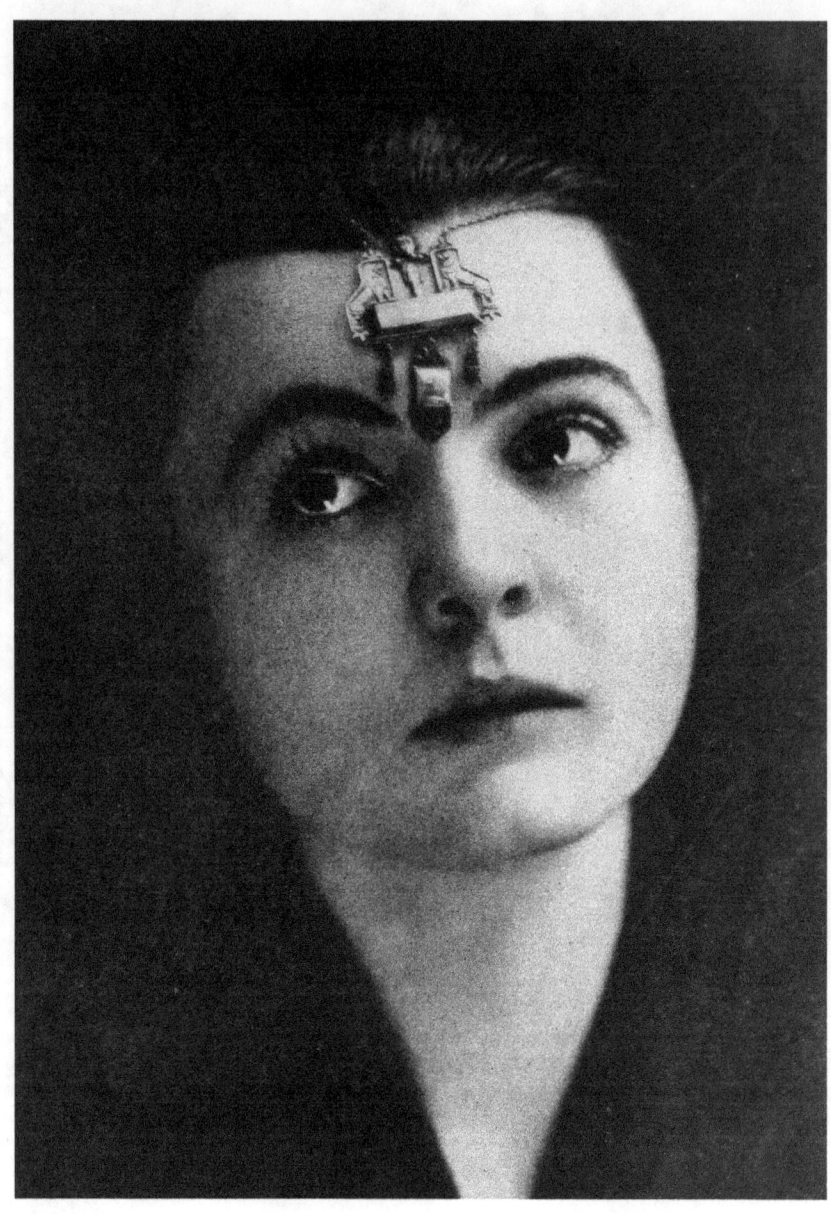

Photo courtesy the Media History Digital Library.

FILE #75869: OLGA GREY

REAL NAME: Anna Zacsek
DOB: November 10, 1896 – New York City
HAIR: dark brown
EYES: dark brown
WANTED FOR: flagrant moral offenses – Note: will be own counsel
ON THE RECORD: "I was now drawing pay for acting... so it occurred to me that I had better learn [how]."

BACKGROUND

Anna was the first child born to Stefan and Teresa, Hungarians who immigrated to Manhattan in 1892. Stefan worked as a janitor, while Teresa cared for her daughter and son Stefan Jr. (1899-1919) in their Park Avenue apartment. (Stefan Jr. died at age 20 from ptomaine poisoning.) Stefan's job as a metal shop foreman allowed them to send the kids to classes at both the L.A. Conservatory of Music & Art and the Egan Institute of Dramatic Art, which counted Marguerite de la Motte, Carmel Myers, Helen Jerome Eddy, and Carol Dempster among its pupils. Anna's April 1910 stage debut was with the Lyric Theatre Stock Company in *Children of the Ghetto*. Audiences loved her! She had "it" and everybody noticed, especially Majestic, who made her an extra when she and Dad visited the studio in 1914-1915.

[Note: I chose to stick with Anna everywhere other than the film section, since that's the only time she used that name.]

MOVING PICTURES: SCHOOLS OF IMMORALITY

His Lesson (Mutual, 1915): Olga is the surprisingly uncredited "Dorothy Vernon" in her first film, a romantic drama starring George Siegmann as Bat, a street tough trying to go straight, and Billie West as Mamie, his frail sweetheart. Dorothy sets Bat on the straight and narrow, and she and Mamie are rescued by Bat during the film's climax, a terrible fire. Reviews were nothing spectacular, but the entire cast was praised for "naturalness" in "this day of antiquated artificiality" (!)

The Birth of a Nation (Epoch, 1915): Olga (again uncredited) played Laura Keene, onstage in *Our American Cousin* at Ford's Theater the night

Lincoln was shot. (The real-life Keene cradled Lincoln's head as he lay dying; her bloodstained dress cuff is on display at the National Museum of American History.)

The Absentee (Mutual, 1915): This unusual "allegorical drama" introduced concepts in its first half, then segued into a story demonstrating them in action. In the Prologue, "Success leaves Might in charge of his affairs and goes off with Pleasure. Might, influenced by Extravagance and Vanity, forces the Toilers to suffer. Justice tells Success, who returns and ends the misery." The drama revolves around workers' rights in a hat factory: Success is Nathaniel Crosby (Robert Edeson), the company owner; Might, Sampson Rhodes (Allan Sears), the general manager; Vanity is Genevieve Rhodes (Juanita Hansen); Justice is Ruth Farwell (Grey), Nathaniel's stenographer. Mildred Harris as "Innocence," was censored in some locales. It was a noble effort, "skillfully produced," but suffered from sluggish pacing.

Double Trouble (Triangle, 1915): Florian Amidon (Douglas Fairbanks) is clonked on the head and doesn't awaken until five years later. With the help of clairvoyant Madame Leclaire (Grey), he discovers he's spent the last half-decade in Bakerstown as Eugene Brassfield, brash young oil man nominated for mayor and engaged to Elizabeth Waldron (Margery Wilson). The recovery of the timid Amidon renders Brassfield's business a chaotic mess, so she brings back Brassfield – whose idea of fixing things is framing someone else and taking up with Daisy (Gladys Brockwell). Madame essentially vacillates between the two men until everything is cleaned up and Amidon and Waldron can marry. *Moving Picture World* thought it the perfect vehicle for Fairbanks' "versatile talents" but felt Olga's role could've stood a little more development.

Macbeth (Triangle, 1916) was the first American film of Sir Herbert Beerbohm Tree, renowned for the Scottish play on the London stage. Constance Collier also reprised her stage role as Lady MacBeth. Additional cast included Spottiswoode Aitken, Mary Alden, Ralph Lewis, and Olga as Lady Agnes. According to Kevin Brownlow, Tree ran through ALL his dialogue, not grasping the "silent" part of silent film. Rather than insult him, director John Emerson and cinematographer Victor Fleming removed the film from the camera and kept cranking until he was done. Too prestigious for John Q. Public, *Variety* doubted: "Shakespeare on the screen will never have any great vogue."

Intolerance (Triangle, 1916): Olga played "The Adulteress" in the Galilean story, juxtaposing Christ's maltreatment against three other stories of, well, intolerance: The French story, about the St. Bartholomew's Day Massacre, starring Margery Wilson as "Brown Eyes"; The Babylonian story, featuring Constance Talmadge as the feisty "Mountain Girl"; and the Modern story, with Mae Marsh as "The Dear One" and Bobby Harron as "The Boy" amidst the background of crime, poverty, and workers' rights. Griffith created the masterpiece as a response to criticism against his *Birth of a Nation* (1915); he felt victimized, however, and it was not an apology for the former. Olga was listed in reviews as Mary Magdalene, often conflated with the unnamed adulteress, and many said it was the first instance of said character onscreen. Evidently, they'd already forgotten Alice Hollister in *From the Manger to the Cross* (1913). Griffith's vamp, they explained, needed no publicity and shunned the usual stunts like "automobile accidents or airplane adventure" (was this a dig at Carmen Phillips?).

Jim Bludso (Triangle, 1917): Jim Bludso (Wilfred Lucas) returns from the Civil War to find his wife Gabrielle (Grey) has left and taken their son, Little Breeches (Georgie Stone). He finds solace with Kate (Winifred Westover), the storekeeper's daughter, until Gabrielle returns, deserted by her own lover. Meanwhile, crooked contractor Merrill (Sam De Grasse) destroys his own faulty levee and blames the resulting disaster on Jim. Gabrielle is gravely injured in the flood, but manages with her dying breaths to identify Merrill as her former lover. The film culminates in a Bludso-Merrill brawl aboard "The Prairie Belle," ending in an explosion from which only Bludso survives and begins a new life with Kate. Tod Browning wrote the scenario, based on the John Hay poem, and co-directed along with Wilfred Lucas. "[T]his picture holds you with gripping force ... sure to hold the audience," said the *New York Clipper*, who also felt Olga gave "capital support."

The Girl at Home (Paramount, 1917): "[C]heap and trivial" cautionary tale of Jimmie Dexter (Jack Pickford), at school thanks to funding by the generous Padgates, who squanders the money on a sexy and attentive cabaret singer (Grey). His mother (Edythe Chapman) and Jean Padgate (Vivian Martin) visit to chastise him; he takes offense, and earns everything back (plus forgiveness) via tough physical labor. *Variety* liked Olga as the "'vampire' cabaret woman" but thought everything else "mediocre ... [it] should have never been released."

Trixie from Broadway (Pathé, 1919): Chorus girl Trixie (Margarita Fisher) refuses the fancy stage door Johnnies to marry John Collins (Emory Johnson), who turns out to be a millionaire. After overhearing that Trixie married him for his money, he arranges an elaborate ruse (in a dilapidated shack, no less) to test her motives. Gertie (Grey), John's former flame, tries to get Trixie carted off by the Committee on Public Morals, and the resulting catfight sparks a fire; Trixie almost dies saving Gertie, and regains consciousness – and romance – in Collins' mansion. Marred by "forced" situations and shallow characterizations; *Film Daily* regarded it "too artificial to be rated as a good picture."

Olga's last screen project was *The Third Eye* (Pathé, 1920), a 15-chapter mystery serial featuring Warner Oland as the leader of a "murderous" gang, Eileen Percy as the "motion picture star" he desires for his own, and the search for a film reel containing some pretty unsavory activity. The "third eye" is the camera that captured it, cranked by an unknown hand. Olga is the provocative Zaida Savoy, one of the baddies in Oland's crew "concoct[ing] evil plots." *Moving Picture World* enjoyed the "well-woven" story with "suspense in every foot of film."

OTHER SORDID DETAILS

Anna was beautiful: "tall, well built, slim, dark and agile," said the fan magazines. They enjoyed connecting her to the Huns, often fibbing that she was born in Hungary. They also boasted her mastery of violin and piano and the studio school she created at Triangle, offering Montessori-style programs along with French and Italian. Margery Wilson, exceptional herself in a variety of fields, always remembered the "talented Hungarian girl" with whom she'd shared a dressing room.

After motion pictures, Anna returned to the stage and the Little Theater. She performed in several Ibsen plays from late 1920-early 1921, with *Hedda Gabler* selected for matinees at the Morosco in New York City. By spring she was back with Egan in Maeterlinck's *Monna Vanna*, including a command performance for Mary Garden, "especially interested in seeing the work of the young actress." She was the female lead in *The Jest*, one of John and Lionel Barrymore's most successful plays in New York, when it made its Berkeley debut in May 1921.

Teresa Zacsek was in the newspapers that July after police arrested Erma Shief, newsstand vendor, for receipt of stolen property. The property in question was expensive jewelry stolen from Ella Alvord by James Gordon, an itinerant musician, and sold to an unnamed source. Gordon was jailed, and though Anna was initially pegged as the mysterious buyer, further investigation revealed it was Teresa – working a scam with Erma, her sister. The two insisted they were long-estranged, reconciling in court with much weeping and hand-holding, but the law didn't buy it. Anna didn't attend the trial but sent a Note: "pray[ed] all night for your vindication." Thanks to the defense portraying them as victims of the charming Gordon, and their good community standing, they were both acquitted in October.

Anna eloped with actor Arnold Samberg in December 1921, and their official date was February 4, 1922. The marriage was over barely two weeks later. Under the names Arnold Gregg/Arnold Gray, he acted in adventure dramas and Westerns opposite Bessie Barriscale and Seena Owen, and did uncredited work in *The Most Dangerous Game* (1932), *King Kong* (1933), *Twentieth Century* (1934), and *She* (1935). His most famous roles were Arthur the iceman in W.C. Fields' *The Dentist* (1932) and Walker in the Joel McCrea-Dolores Del Rio flick *Bird of Paradise* (1932). On the latter, he met Del Rio's stand-in Josefina Ramos, and the two were married until their deaths four days apart in 1936. (Joel McCrea covered all costs for their double funeral and burial at Hollywood Forever Cemetery.)

She toured Europe, performing in Paris, Vienna, and Budapest, then returned in September 1923 eager to reprise her New York stint under Egan's management. She stayed active on the stage throughout the rest of the 1920s, spending 1924-1926 in New York City in shows like *Carnival* with Elsie Ferguson, then repertoire in Detroit. She met Nazimova while on Broadway and considered her a "great and real source of inspiration." Plans for a partnership with Frank Egan dissolved with his sudden death in 1927; she put together the Actor's Theater herself. By the end of the decade she was part of the Los Angeles Opera & Drama Guild and reprised her role in *Monna Vanna* alongside Boris Karloff as her husband.

Life on the boards soured, culminating in a 1929 lawsuit against her darling Egan Theater for salaries owed; they'd withheld her payment for *Hotel Imperial* due to insufficient ticket sales. She won the case, but was tired and disillusioned. "I cannot go one forever on the stage," she confessed to a friend one night at dinner. Her friend suggested she study law, and Anna warmed to the idea. She attended Loyola University Law School and passed the bar in December 1932. Primarily a defense attorney, she took on several interesting cases including that of Grace du Bois, an elderly woman from an aristocratic family line who murdered her son because he was "too noble to live" (Anna lost, du Bois sentenced to life in prison) and Pedro Gonzalez, one of the first Spanish-speaking radio announcers, railroaded by the Los Angeles Police Department for his controversial views. Anna got a confession from the woman coerced into filing a false rape report, but the judge refused new testimony and Gonzalez remained in jail. (He was deported in 1940.) At one point she was one of only two practicing female attorneys in Los Angeles.

Her biggest case was defending Henry Leyvas, Victor Segobia, and Edward Grandpré in the incendiary Sleepy Lagoon Murder Trial. Ostensibly about the death of Jose Diaz, it was a racist attack on "Pachucos" and Mexican-American youth culture of the 1940s in general. Seventeen young men (including Leyvas) were arrested and held without bail; despite a lack of evidence, nine were convicted of murder and sent to San Quentin, the rest (on lesser charges) to the Los Angeles County Jail. Continuing tensions around the case exploded into a week-long 1943 riot between white residents, particularly servicemen, and young Mexican-Americans, Blacks, and Filipino-Americans, labeled the "Zoot Suit Riots." Anna also served as divorce attorney to famed architect Rudolph Schindler. She was introduced to him by mutual friend, photographer Edward Weston, and they formed a close (some say sexual) relationship. Schindler did the sets for several of Anna's productions, including the ill-fated *Hotel Imperial*, and designed a home for her on Playa del Rey in 1936.

She lived with the now-divorced Teresa on Sunset Blvd. until 1945, when she married Orlando Weber Jr. The son of Orlando Weber Sr., chairman and co-founder of Allied Chemical & Dye Corp., he was previously married to artist Irene Bohus, friend of Frida Kahlo and lover to Diego Rivera. The multimillionaire Weber was a stage actor (under the name "Kevin Kemble"), poet, pianist, artist, horticulturist, and "ballet-o-mane." He was also a *wunderkind* in the world of ornithology, leading an expedition to Venezuela when he was only seventeen. They were living separately when Weber, 33, died of an overdose in his Park Avenue apartment in September of 1953. His will, after charity stipulations, left everything to chauffeur/valet/secretary Rodney Vaale. (Anna previously waived her interest in his estate after he established a "living trust" for her.) Vaale, Weber's "dear friend," attempted suicide by overdose in December 1959, and succeeded in May 1960. I suspect their relationship was more than just friendship, and I also believe Anna knew and understood. On Weber's headstone in Calvary Cemetery there's a haunting poem, author unknown, which ends: "I buried you, my love, beneath the grass / Never dreaming this would come to pass."

Anna's address by 1948 was 211 South Muirfield Road in Los Angeles, known as the Fudger home. The "palatial" Spanish colonial had quite the pedigree: Howard Hughes lived there during 1926-1942, the productive period spawning *Hell's Angels* (1930), *The Front Page* (1931), and *Scarface* (1932). He shared the home with wife Ella, then Billie Dove and Katharine Hepburn following his divorce. Schindler made a few modifications for her, and she remained there the rest of her life.

Her third husband, Istvan Kopcso, came to the United States in 1956 as part of Operation Safe Haven I. Sponsored by the "Hungarian Relief Operation" (Dec 1956-June 1957), it relocated 35,000 refugees who had fled to Austria after their uprising was crushed by the USSR. They traveled by train or bus to Munich, Germany, then flown to McGuire AFB in New Jersey and "processed for settlement" at Camp Kilmer. Kopcso, who later changed his name to Stephen Windsor, was 39; she was 63. They were married until her death.

CASE CLOSED

Anna Zacsek died in Los Angeles, CA on April 25, 1973 due to atrial fibrillation, cerebral thrombosis, and peritonitis resulting from a perforated intraabdominal viscus. She was cremated at Shimatsu-Ogata-Kubota Mortuary and interred at the Oddfellows Cemetery, San Francisco, CA. Anna was 75.

MUGSHOTS

Fresh-faced Anna. Photo courtesy the Media History Digital Library.

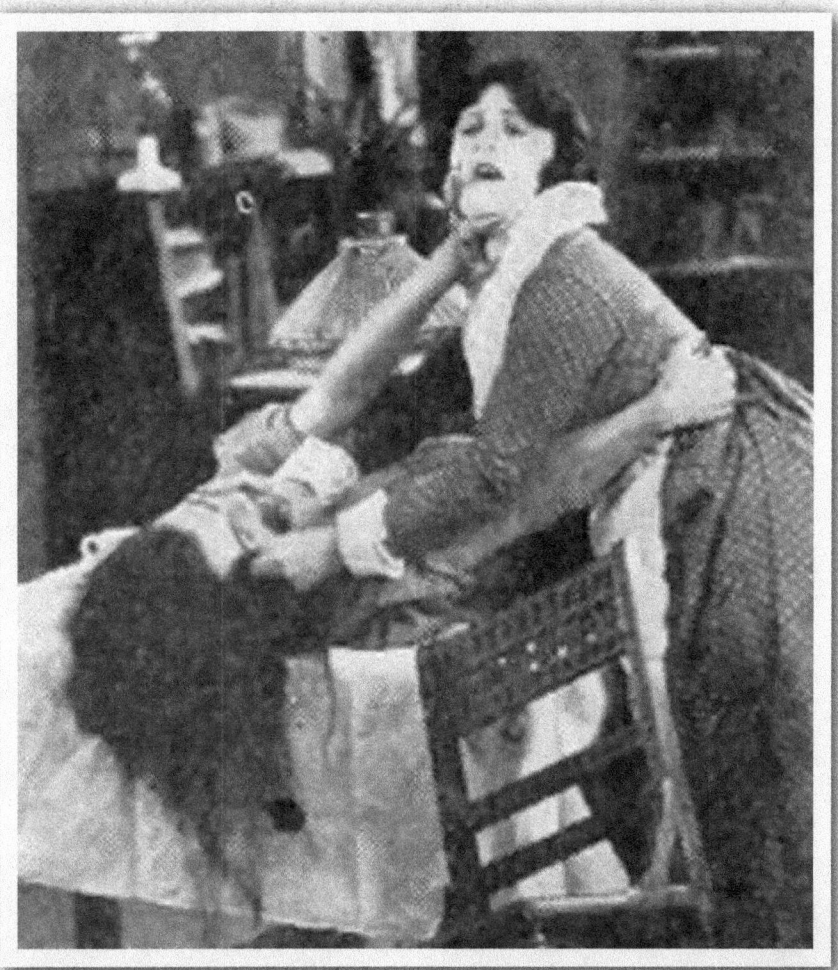

A scene from Trixie from Broadway *(1919). Photo courtesy the Media History Digital Library.*

Photo courtesy Peter J. Fox.

FILE #13971: ROSA RUDAMI

REAL NAME: Rosalia Governali
DOB: December 6 or 11, 1898 – New York City
HAIR: "raven-black"
EYES: black
WANTED FOR: well, they called her "The Killer," so ....
ON THE RECORD: "We shall see, my friend, if Rudami ever bends her head in homage to any."

BACKGROUND

Of all the vamps in these files, Rosa's background is arguably the most tempestuous. She was the first child born to Pietro Governali and Francesca Damico. Pietro hailed from Palermo, Sicily, and emigrated to NY in 1889, where he met fellow Italian immigrant Francesca. They wed in 1896, and by 1900 lived with their baby daughter and Pietro's two younger sisters on East 13th Street in New York City. The Governalis had six more children, only three of whom survived: Julia (1904-2007), Diana (1906-2000), and Philip (1908-1958). Pietro, the only one who could read and write in English, supported his growing family in varying ways, from grocer to courier to barber. Rosina helped out by singing professionally during her teenage years. Five years later, Pietro and Diana worked at the New Jersey Worsted Spinning Company and Julia at a nearby embroidery company, after the whole family moved to Garfield, NJ. Well, except for one ...

August 21, 1919: a young lady knelt on the steps of St. Patrick's Cathedral and swallowed a bottle of iodine. A passing patrolman rushed her to the hospital; the dosage is not lethal. The girl, who gave the name Rosina González Gamarra, spun a painful tale of love and loss during her arraignment on attempted suicide charges. She was madly in love with a cartoonist who, after a year of "association," claimed he'd "outgrown" her and called off their wedding. Rosina was inconsolable. "There was only one thing left to do ... I am sorry I failed to die."

November 1, 1919: Rosina, fully recovered, marries Maurice Rudomine, a fur trimmer from France and brother of celebrated photographer Albert Rudomine. "My husband knew about the artist," she said, "but vowed he loved me just the same." The two took an apartment on West 95th Street. One week later, on November 8, Rosina passed out in the subway station at 50th and Broadway. She was rushed to Bellevue, where an empty iodine bottle and clippings about the August incident were found in her pockets. Tears rolled down her olive cheeks as she lay in her hospital bed: "I don't want to live anymore." Rudomine, an "anarchist," left her after three days of marriage. "He thought I would help him in the cause ... when I would not agree he [called] me a 'dirty conventionalist'." Rosina tried to jump out the window, but he yanked her back in; "[t]hen I took the poison and followed him out of the house." She again wept over the artist who had "pretended" to love her and ruined her life. After she regained strength, her mother and sister Diana brought her home to Garfield. Rosina's son, Peter, was born July 30, 1920, after which she joined her sister and father at the mill. Questions remained: Who was this artist, and what was the name Rosina gave during her arraignment?

Francisco González Gamarra (1890-1972) was an artist from Cuzco, Peru. In the late 1910s he lived on West 38th Street in Manhattan and worked for the *New York Herald-Tribune*, which published his political cartoons. He excelled at music and sculpture, but it was his oil paintings celebrating indigenous Peruvian culture that earned back-to-back exhibitions, first in Washington D.C, then at the Museum of Natural History in New York. In 1928 he received the Order del Sol, one of the highest awards in Peru, for his "positive diffusion of Peruvian culture." Gamarra wrote "The Theory of Peruvian Art" in 1937, a list of ten points essential to its creation, but distilled them into only one: "It is to love Peru." His music and art are still taught in Peruvian schools, and he was recognized as one of the "four greats of Cuzco" in 1995.

Rosa's 1923 divorce suit against Rudomine revealed more details about their brief but tumultuous marriage. She'd doubted his fidelity since their wedding day; like many anarchists of the time, he was a proponent of "free love" and wanted Rosa to participate. "He actually brought one man into the room," she said, "introduced me as his sweetheart and not as his wife and told the man he could go with me." Rumors swirled about him and Esther Chambers, a dressmaker living on Lexington Avenue, the same block where Rosa had a tea-room. (At the time, while studying voice and drama, Rosa supported herself with two successful cafés in the city, one catering almost solely to students attending the School of Art and Design.) One day she and three friends rang Chambers' doorbell, and a drunk Rudomine in his undershirt slammed the door in their faces. Rosa and her crew returned later and found Rudomine "sitting on a cot with Miss Chambers' head in his lap." One of Rosa's friends attacked Rudomine, then Chambers; there was much screaming and hair-pulling and the cops showed up, but Rosa sent them away, having "obtained the evidence she desired." Rudomine, ever the gentleman, felt reconciliation between him and his wife possible, with one stipulation: she'd have to "give it away," the "it" being baby Peter, whom he'd never met. You could imagine Rosa's reaction to this. (She won the suit and got full custody.)

MOVING PICTURES: SCHOOLS OF IMMORALITY

The Masked Dancer (Principal, 1924): Trade papers mentioned "Rosina Rudami" in the cast, playing an "East Indian," but she wasn't in the credits. The film starred Lowell Sherman, Helene Chadwick, and Leslie Austen in a comedy-drama not unlike 1931's *Madam Satan*: housewife transforms into mysterious masked dancer to reignite her tepid husband.

Other films in which Rosa allegedly appears but is absent from credits include the Pauline Garon-David Powell drama *The Average Woman* (C.C. Burr, 1924) and *It Is the Law* (Fox, 1924), a mystery starring Arthur Hohl and Herbert Heyes. (Both films also contained bit roles for De Sacia Mooers.) There was buzz that Rosa had signed with FBO for a series of six pictures, but in April/May 1925 she officially joined Leatrice Joy, Julia Faye, Jetta Goudal, and Sally Rand as a member of Cecil B. DeMille's stock company.

The Wedding Song (Producers Distributing Corp., 1925): Hayes Hallan (Robert Ames) is young, rich, and marrying the lovely Beatrice (Leatrice Joy). He doesn't know that Beatrice is working with her family of crooks to scam him out of his fortune. Lucky for Hallan, Beatrice falls in love and turns on the ne'er-do-wells, saving her husband from a bomb that ultimately sinks the crooks' boat. Rosa played Ethea, "a Hawaiian girl" who "twice tried to stab Leatrice Joy and finally shot her." Film Daily liked its "unusual twists" despite a draggy ending.]

The central film in DeMille's list of upcoming films was *The Volga Boatman* (1926), a romance of the Russian Revolution starring William Boyd and Elinor Fair along with many of his stock players (Rosa included). Two others due in 1926: *Made for Love*, a Leatrice Joy romance of Egypt, archaeology, and reincarnation, and *Three Faces East*, a WWI spy drama starring Jetta Goudal and Henry B. Walthall. Early press for the Joy picture gleefully promised Rosa "ruined three families with an automatic."

DeMille and Rosa often battled for "supremacy" on-set and by February 1926 decided to part ways. "You'll be back," said one employee. "He'll break your spirit ... and then make you a great star." An amused Rosa allegedly replied, "Mr. DeMille [was] fortunate to be permitted an interest in Rosa Rudami's career." In response, DeMille cut all her scenes from his 1926 releases; the role of Mariusha the "gypsy" who "killed three men" – most likely Rosa's part – went to Julia Faye. "Now [Rudami] prefers to free lance [sic]," read one terse release.

A Poor Girl's Romance (FBO, 1926): Wealthy Wellington Kingston (Creighton Hale) saves Anne (Gertrude Short) from hoodlums. Later, a guest catches her watching a society ball from outside and drags her in as a joke. Kingston, in attendance, prevents her ridicule by calling her "Princess Anne." The jealous Madeline (Rudami) exposes the lie and Anna gets tossed out. Time passes and Anne is now a Fifth Avenue model for Theodore Chappell, Madeline's beau. One night after dinner with friends (including Kingston), Chappell is shot. Anne confesses in a mistaken attempt to protect Kingston, but he and a cabdriver both witnessed Madeline pull the trigger. The correct murderer is caught and Kingston and Anne's romance begins. "An up-to-the-minute story of the love of a society man and a beautiful girl of the slums [with] a fine cast," said the *Tampa Bay Times*. Rosa made personal appearances across California to promote the film; "several Italian artists" performed a musical program at one engagement. A nineteen-year-old violinist and budding composer wrote "Just for You" specifically for the picture, and the song was a "big hit in the Los Angeles supper clubs and dance halls." His name was Russell Colombo." [Rudami] literally gave Russ Columbo to the world," said columnist Jimmie Fidler. "[H]e was her chauffeur and errand boy ... Rosa helped him obtain his first professional job with an orchestra" at the Montmartre Cafe in Hollywood, where legend says he learned to sing. From 1931-1934 he, Rudy Vallee, and Bing Crosby were in a three-way tie for favorite crooner, the self-composed "Prisoner of Love" his signature song. He was involved with Carole Lombard at the time of his death from an accidental gunshot wound at age 26.

The Lily (Fox, 1926): The first screen version of Belasco's success adapted from Garoux's "Le Lys," starring Belle Bennett in the Nance O'Neil role. A romance of a daughter who generously gives up her life in order to care for her selfish father (John St. Polis) and protect her younger sister (Reata Hoyt), but is rewarded by true love in the end, from the incredibly patient family lawyer (Richard Tucker). Rosa's role is unclear but decidedly minor. Reviews were mostly good, with Bennett singled out as "superb," though some found the "deep and heavy" material made for slow, "stilted" going.

Afterwards, papers had Rosa splitting time between stage and screen, or making those in the Algonquin "sit up and take notice" with her jet black ultra-long hair. She signed a contract to do four "talkies" with Halperin Productions in 1928, but no further films followed.

OTHER SORDID DETAILS

With that hair (a reported member of the "anti-bob" brigade), those "languorous" eyes, and skin "the color of bronze," she resembled "one of

Raphael's Madonnas" more than a sadistic homewrecker. She impressed columnist Isabel Stuyvesant with her self-designed couture; one "ravishing" black and white satin gown was "fashioned like a calla lily," while another allegedly won first prize at an International Artists' Association contest in New York.

The Sicilian beauty inspired numerous sobriquets. "The Black Orchid." "The Killer," due to all her onscreen stabbing and shooting. David Warfield christened her "The Girl with the Midnight Eyes" after *The Merchant of Venice* (1922) at the Lyceum in New York City. A San Francisco doorman, not to be outdone, came up with "The Girl with the Queer Eyes." The *Los Angeles Times* attempted "the Latin Lillian Gish" but it never caught on.

Cecil B. DeMille claimed Rosa was a "leading lady of the Italian Theater in New York." (He also made her a secret service agent working undercover in Massachusetts, and that's why publicity profiles require many, many grains of salt.) The Italian-American Immigrant Theater began in the 1870s and, like the much-celebrated Yiddish theater of the time, presented professional talent in original plays, opera arias, and Shakespeare translated into dialect. It flourished between 1900 and 1924, the year U.S. immigration quotas went into effect. Rosa was said to have been in shows like *Zaza, Madame X*, and *A Daughter of Destiny*.

She possessed the stately bearing of a queen. "[H]er confidence is colossal," wrote Myrtle Gebhart for *Picture-Play*. According to the article, her apartment was appropriately exotic, with "Persian chests," "alabaster jars filled with pungent scents" (shades of Mary Magdalene?) and boxes of heavy gold jewelry. The magazine humanized her with remarks about her fervent Catholicism and charity work with handicapped children, but it wasn't puffery: Rosa's life revolved around philanthropy. In 1925 she begged clemency from Governor Smith of New York for eighteen-year-old Angelina Tavano, nurse to the son of City Judge Leo Minkin. She kidnapped the three-year-old in 1923 and was subsequently sentenced to prison. Rosa argued for leniency, basing Tavano's crime on the indescribable pain (and resulting drug habit) from losing her own child three years earlier. Besides, she and Leo Jr. adored each other, and there was never any intent to harm him. Rosa's efforts gained Tavano an appeal, and her sentence amended to Bedford Hills Reformatory, where training and care prepared her for a changed life upon release. Later that same year, knowing "what it means to be lonely," she hosted Thanksgiving dinner for 32 needy newsboys at Brandstatter's Piccadilly. She provided music, entertainment, and a box of candy for each boy.

In 1928, someone found a newborn in the backseat of an "expensive automobile" and rushed the baby to the hospital, where the mother was identified as Dorothy Nolan. The 21-year-old telephone operator, unwed and with only 22¢ to her name, chose the car hoping its owner would provide her child with a better life. Upon hearing of Nolan's arrest for desertion (and perhaps feeling a pang of kinship with the girl) Rosa hired her a lawyer, got her released, set her up with a job and proper wardrobe, and got her baby back.

Rosa married "young Chicago millionaire" John Conway Fox at Agua Caliente that September after a three-week courtship. Fox was an architect, writer, and real estate operator related to John Fox Jr., author of the 1908 novel *The Trail of The Lonesome Pine*. A church wedding followed in October, and he happily adopted Peter as his own. He wasn't the only one with interesting relatives: two years earlier Rosa threw a big party for her cousin Josephine Lucchese, prima donna of the San Francisco Opera Co., when she visited Los Angeles on tour. Lots of Hollywood attended to fete the "American Nightingale," including Francis X. Bushman, Lenore Coffee, Anita Stewart, and Sylvia Breamer. Lucchese later performed with the Roxy Ensemble in the early 1930s under the name Mata Cora.

John's family and Rosa clashed immediately. His father died in 1927, and his mother refused to provide an account of John Sr.'s estate. Rosa (on behalf of her husband) sued for an injunction barring her mother-in-law and her new husband, optician William Beek, from "dispos[al] of heirlooms at auction" in order to undervalue the $20 million estate. The Beeks, who estimated it at $100,000, laughed off the suit as a clear-cut case of a "disappointed gold seeker." "Wait until the pretty wife learns the truth," chuckled Mr. Beek. While info about the case's resolution is vague, both the Beeks and John Fox Jr. were ordered to sell off Palm Beach property by the Continental Illinois Bank & Trust Co.

The Foxes remained in West Palm Beach through 1929 and owned the Piccadilly Grill for a time. They were back in Garfield by 1930, living with Julia, her bank clerk husband, Tom, and their son Leonard. John worked as a magazine editor, and Rosa noticed something alarming: her eyesight, a problem since her days with DeMille, was failing. Swift intervention arrested the damage, and she and John "jumped together into the hurly-burly of antique dealing" in 1933. Rosa, wearing thick Coke-bottle glasses, ran Manhattan Galleries in the Sherry-Netherland Hotel, NYC, a shop for collectors and those who just want "nice things for their homes." They crossed the globe hunting for treasures, and even bought some of Belasco's own pieces from the 17th century.

They made their home in Manhattan by the late 1930s/early 1940s. Rosa was an interior decorator, while Fox and son Peter worked in building and advising capacities for the State of New York in Albany. Peter served in WWII, rose to the rank of sergeant, and married Gwendolyn Smith in 1944. From the 1940s on, following a move to Albany, Rosa worked indefatigably in social work, particularly for Italian-Americans and those of Puerto Rican descent. She never forgot the sometimes suffocating cultural atmosphere of her youth – "[young Italian women] must ask permission of their parents for anything they wish to do. They must be accompanied by a relative when they go out in the evening . . . they live, let me remind you, in this country." She founded the United Form of Italian-American Women in the United States. She was named adult education supervisor in the State Education Dept., providing guidance and "civilian defense training" for those born outside the U.S. She lectured and wrote on the need for naturalization work. Rosa, who spoke five languages, frequently traveled to Puerto Rico, her work predating statehood; she was the first woman sent there to develop educational programs for residents coming to the United States. When she retired in 1959, she was honored with a banquet and the Amita award for "assisting schools and community inter-action [sic] among aliens, non-English speaking illiterates, semi-literates, and unaided workers." War brides, refugees, displaced people looking for citizenship: Rosa helped them long before public programs became the norm.

CASE CLOSED

Rosa Rudami died of pneumonia in Albany, NY on February 3, 1966. Bishop Edward Maginn, apostolic administrator for the Albany Catholic Diocese, personally said her requiem mass in gratitude for her lifelong work with the immigrant community. Interment was at the historic St. Agnes Cemetery in Menands, NY. She was 67.

MUGSHOTS

Elegant Rosa. Photo courtesy Peter J. Fox.

Scene from The Wedding Song *(1925). Photo courtesy Peter J. Fox.*

Photo courtesy the Media History Digital Library.

FILE #85948: ROSEMARY THEBY

REAL NAME: Rosemary Therése Theby
DOB: April 8, 1892 – St. Louis, MO
HAIR: black
EYES: hazel
WANTED FOR: corruption of clergy
ON THE RECORD: "Fighting for your rights as a woman are as nothing compared with the energy with which you have to fight to be versatile as a screen actress."

BACKGROUND

Rosemary was the middle child born to Louis Theby, "laborer" at various jobs, and Katherine "Kate" Masering. She had one older brother, Louis Jr. (1890-1953), and one younger brother Arthur (1899-1912). The family lived on Garfield Avenue in St. Louis by 1910 census, Louis a factory-employed shoe cutter, "Rosa" a stenographer at a tobacco works, ambitious despite "[l]ittle opportunity for educational advantages."

Her (alleged) discovery story, as told by former boss J.E. Stewart Sr.: Rosemary stepped in one day when the cashier was absent; the customer, a "motion picture man from New York," invited the pretty young lady to be an extra on set. After the shoot ended the director remarked on her "latent ability." Her mother and friends (what about Dad?) advised her to explore acting, so she moved "absolutely alone" to New York and studied for six months at Sargent Dramatic School. Shortly after graduating, "Mr. Thompson of the [sic] Vitagraph offered me a position at the studios on the strength of a fancied resemblance to Mary Fuller, who had just left" for Edison and eventual superstardom.

MOVING PICTURES: SCHOOLS OF IMMORALITY

Rosemary's first role was an uncredited bit alongside Maurice Costello and Florence Turner in *The Sacrifice* (1911), a melodrama of a convict and the daughter he could not raise. After appearing as Celia in *As You Like It* (1912) a year later, trade promos described her as a "pronounced brunette, slightly Oriental... well adapted to heavy leads."

The Reincarnation of Karma (1912) was a lurid amalgam of "Oriental" mysticism. Karma (Courtenay Foote), virtuous Indian high priest, is seduced by the beautiful Quinetrea (Theby). Afterwards, the shame-filled priest curses her and she becomes a giant Freudian snake. 2000 years later, Karma is reincarnated as Leslie Adams (also Foote), and he and heiress fiancée Lillian White (Lillian Walker) visit the ruined ancient temple. They are shocked to find the serpent still lives – and, promptly transforming back into Quinetrea, is hungry for revenge....

The film, touted as the first three-reeler, distressed the public with its eroticism. Chagrined managers deflected numerous complaints; during the 1914 Motion Picture Commission to determine a "decent films" policy, they used *Karma* as the prime example of a contentious picture. *Moving Picture News* felt the "actions of the leading lady ... would put to shame the most shameless coochie-coochie dancer in the most abandoned 'midway'... [t]here are sweet, dainty and fascinating ways of making love in the pictures that could have been employed." Quinetrea wasn't dainty and sweet, but she was memorable, and, thanks to her, Rosemary was too.

In June 1913 she moved to Reliance, debuting "in her familiar role of the heartless adventuress" as Leone St. Regis in *The Tangled Web* (1913). After approximately fifteen films at Reliance she departed for Lubin and *A Question of Right* (1914) costarring Harry C. Myers. She played against type as Louise Gray, the innocent beauty who marries a mayor only to find out he is "a grafter and a scoundrel." They had great chemistry, which Lubin channeled into a series of popular "domestic comedies". When Lubin folded, they went to Universal's Victor division; then Vim after they bought out bankrupt Lubin, and when Vim went under, back to Universal until Pathé picked the series up. Myers often directed and sometimes wrote the Myers-Theby Comedies, which shunned slapstick for "refined" situational humor: unexpected houseguests, mothers-in-law, even the mumps (though acting while one's mouth is stuffed full of cotton sounds like a Sennett gag). Audiences enjoyed watching them, and the pair enjoyed making them. "I feel my best work has been done under the direction of Harry C. Meyers [sic]," Rosemary told columnist Caroline Carr. "He is both my director and my leading man. [W]orking under Mr. Meyers [sic] makes the many hardships ... seem small compared to his kindness and consideration." Most folks thought they were married in real life, but nowhere was an offscreen romance mentioned.

After the newlywed comedies ended, Rosemary freelanced in Lyons-Moran comedies at Nestor and Billy West comedies at King Bee; the "vamp" role in Griffith's *The Great Love* (1918) for Paramount; and a couple of serials: Francis Ford's *The Silent Mystery* (1918) and *The Mystery Of 13* (1919). From 1919 to 1924 she made over fifty films. Here are some notable ones:

Upstairs and Down (Selznick-Select, 1919) was based on the 1916 hit Broadway comedy about "the idle rich and their loose morals." Alice Chesterson (Olive Thomas) is tired of boring fiancé Tom Carey (David Butler) and takes up with Irish playboy Terrence O'Keefe (Robert Ellis). After they're caught together at the "Midnight Frolic" Alice begs her sister Betty (Theby) to do damage control. Betty arranges a car "wreck" where Terrence can find her, and the two fall in love. Alice, jealous instead of grateful, lies that Terrence "ruined" her. He forces her to confess; Tom, newly encouraged, becomes the dominant male Alice always wanted. Oh, and Betty and Terrence plan their future wedding. All this happens under the watchful eyes of the house servants, going through romantic machinations of their own. *Upstairs and Down* largely invented the "baby vamp," and Olive Thomas owned the role; it was silly, soap-opera fun, meant to "give almost everybody a few laughs and then they will forget about it."

Terror Island (Paramount, 1920): Harry Harper (Houdini) invents a submarine, and Beverly West (Lila Lee) begs him to use it to free her father, captive on a South Sea island. The natives want the special pearl Beverly own, but so does her uncle and guardian (Wilton Taylor), who kidnaps her. Beverly is thrown overboard several times – once in an iron safe! – but Harry dependably rescues her while fighting off her other greedy, ne'er-do-well relatives (Eugene Pallette and Theby). He then impresses the natives with magic tricks, who graciously release Mr. West, and the three life happily . . . well, you know. Houdini movies weren't exactly known for realism, but even by those standards *Terror Island* was farfetched. "Chances are pretty big that this will get laughed at," said *Film Daily*. "[The film] is awfully rude to an audience's sense of plausibility." Worst of all, despite all the rescues and safes, not one of Houdini's famous "liberating stunts" is shown on camera!

Kismet (Robertson-Cole, 1920) is all about Otis Skinner. The legendary stage actor's "gorgeous" first screen appearance is as Hajj the beggar, the character he created on Broadway. He made only one other movie, a sound version of *Kismet* (First National, 1930) with Loretta Young. We follow Hajj as he cheats, steals, attempts murder, escapes from prison, saves his daughter Marsinah (Elinor Fair) from a harem and its queen, Kut-al-Kulub (Theby), and makes a pilgrimage to Mecca – all in the course of 24 hours. The film ends with Hajj falling asleep on the same mosque steps where he awoke that morning. Variety thought "Elinor Fair and Rosemary Theby contrasted youth and jealous disappointment with admirable command." Commendation indeed opposite such a renowned thespian as Skinner.

A Connecticut Yankee at King Arthur's Court (Fox, 1920): Martin Cavendish (Myers) has a problem: his mother wants him to marry Lady Gordon, but he's in love with Mom's secretary Betty (Pauline Starke). One night he's reading the Twain book when a burglar breaks in and knocks him on the head. Cavendish wakes up at the court of King Arthur (Charles Clary), whom he regales with modern slang and teaches about telephones. Merlin (William Mong) thinks him a sorcerer and wants him burned at the stake, but correctly "predicting" an eclipse and rescuing a damsel (Pauline Starke) from the "nasty" Queen Morgan le Fay (Theby) earns back their favor. He caps things off by winning a tournament, wakes up back in 1920, and elopes with Betty. The "fairly spectacular production" was a huge hit for Rosemary and Myers, and the role most associated with him for many years. "[S]ome really good comedy," wrote *Film Daily*, but "someone should give [Myers] some lessons in the art of make-up."

The Girl of the Golden West (First National, 1923) was based on the hit Belasco play, and another vamp role for Rosemary. The Girl (Sylvia Breamer) loves Ramerrez (J. Warren Kerrigan), revealed as an outlaw. She shelters him but "wicked Mexican hussy" Nina (Theby) tips off the sheriff (Russell Simpson), who shoots Ramerrez during his attempted escape. The Girl retrieves and, though failing again to hide him, earns their permanent freedom in a poker game. When the inevitable angry mob, led by the "fiery" Nina, arrives to lynch Ramerrez, the sheriff honors The Girl's hard-won bargain and rescues him. A melodrama to be sure, but a solid one with a strong cast, "splendid entertainment with genuine box office qualities."

Tea—With a Kick! (Associated, 1923): Rosemary was "Aunt Pearl" in this odd little comedy poking fun at Prohibition. The thin plot – Bonnie (Doris May) opens a tea room (read: cabaret), the proceeds of which will spring her framed father from prison – served as an excuse for dancing girls, an all-star cast, and a fashion show "displaying $100,000 worth of Paris modes a year in advance." Louize Fazenda, Snitz Edwards, Chester Conklin, Hank Mann, Zasu Pitts, Ralph Lewis, Creighton Hale ... Others may want *London After Midnight* but this "bright and amusing" film has my vote.

The Red Lily (Metro-Goldwyn, 1924): Homeless Marise La Noue (Enid Bennett) elopes to Paris with Jean Leonnec (Ramón Novarro), the mayor's son. They are separated and Leonnec ends up a thief, La Noue a prostitute. After Leonnec serves a years-long prison sentence, the two, no longer young and optimistic, reunite. Can they surmount their personal changes? "Strong dramatic entertainment ... fine playing of a talented cast, including Rosemary's small yet "individually fine" role of streetwalker Nana.

So Big (First National, 1924) was the first filmed version of Edna Ferber's celebrated novel. Colleen Moore was Selina Peake, a wealthy girl with a promising future until her father dies, penniless, in a gambling den. The newly-destitute Peake starts over as a teacher in a poor prairie town, married to farmer Pervus (John Bowers). Her only light is her son, Dirk, nicknamed "So Big." Pervus dies, and an old friend lends Peake the money to make the farm fruitful again. Dirk (Ben Lyon) thrives thanks to his mother's arduous efforts, until a scandalous affair threatens to ruin his budding architectural career. A terrified Peake begs the woman's husband not to sue, and he relents, clearing the way for Dirk's future success. It was Colleen Moore's personal favorite of all her films and she gave an "electric performance," proving she was an actress "of the highest quality." The rest of the cast reflected the picture's importance, including Gladys Brockwell, Jean Hersholt, Wallace Beery, and Joseph De Grasse among others. Rosemary played Paula Storm, the woman with whom Dirk gets tangled in scandal. According to *Film Daily*, "the long and imposing cast didn't falter for a moment."

Midnight Daddies (Sono Art-World Wide Pictures, 1930) was Mack Sennett's first all-talking comedy. Charlie Mason, *modiste*, runs into his cousin Wilbur Louder (Andy Clyde) and his wife (Theby) one day on the beach. He invites Wilbur to meet him at a café where his models gather, including Camille (Alma Bennett), whom Charlie has tasked with vamping Wilbur out of enough cash to save his nearly bankrupt business. Mrs. Louder reciprocates with dinner, but when Charlie arrives, there's another surprise guest: Camille. Mrs. Louder is no fool, and a drunk Charlie confesses, confirming her suspicions. She forgives her gullible husband and all ends happily. Tepid critical response, but "not bad entertainment."

Ten Nights in a Barroom (State Rights, 1931) was yet another rehashing of the old "meller," produced by the Department of Prohibition Education. Adapted from the extremely popular temperance play (in turn based on Timothy Shay Arthur's 1854 novel), William Farnum is Joe Morgan, ruined by alcohol use encouraged by cruel bar owner Slade (Tom Santschi), who has designs on Morgan's business. It's a bleak look at how addiction destroys both yourself and the lives of your loved ones, in this case his wife (Theby) and the sickly daughter (Peggy Lou Lynd), forced to walk alone through the dark to fetch him from the bar. Farnum overemotes, but it fits the source material. *Harrison's Reports* thought the film "surprisingly effective." They also enjoyed the climax, a protracted fight scene lifted from Farnum and Santschi's famous row in *The Spoilers* (1914), still considered by some to be the best fight sequence ever committed to film.

The Thirties were rocky for Myers-Theby. Myers floated a new series about "average married couples," acquiring an "experienced camera man [sic]" and "ten well known players," but nothing happened. Their star power long since dimmed, they spent the decade in "dress extra roles" and as background atmosphere. In his syndicated "Hollywood" column, Ed Sullivan's fictional extra namechecked the pair, writing in her letter home: "It would really break your heart, Mamma, to see the people in this town who used to be big stars . . . ." Oliver Hardy, an old friend from their Lubin/Vim days, helped them get work; they made comedy shorts at Educational, and played uncredited roles in *San Francisco* (1936), *Vogues Of 1938* (1937), *Make Way for Tomorrow* (1937), and *You Can't Take It with You* (1938). Ironically, during this denouement, the two would make the films they are both remembered for today. She was "Ma Snavely," W.C. Fields' wife, in the hilarious *The Fatal Glass of Beer* (1933). The Yukon comedy spoofed "lesson" films like *Ten Nights in a Barroom*. In Myers' case, it was the "eccentric millionaire" whose rescue leads the Tramp to love and acceptance, in the Chaplin masterpiece *City Lights* (1931). He also popped up in Laurel and Hardy's *Block Heads* (1938) and posthumously with Hardy and Harry Langdon in *Zenobia* (1939).

Rosemary's last film was *One Million B.C.* (United Artists, 1940). Produced by D.W. Griffith, directed by Hal Roach Sr. and Jr, and narrated by Conrad Nagel, this prehistoric Romeo and Juliet story was the year's biggest box-office attraction. Tumak (Victor Mature) of the rough Rock people loves Loana (Carole Landis) of the gentle Shell people; the tribes lock horns until twin dangers (a dinosaur and volcano) spark solidarity. She (billed as Rosemary Thebe) was a Shell person, and several old timers like Ed Coxen, Creighton Hale, and Ricca Allen played Rock or Shell people.

OTHER SORDID DETAILS

The early 1920s were a time of great change for Rosemary. She shared a place for a bit on star-studded Wilcox Avenue in L.A. with comedienne Teddy Sampson, known for her work with (and marriage to) Ford Sterling. She lived sedately, prompting gentle mocking from The *Los Angeles Times*: "She has about as much heavy atmosphere about her as little Mary of the nursery rhyme." She enjoyed cleaning and playing golf, insisting "the more ardently vampier [actresses] are in pictures, the more of a virtuous recluse we want to be when off." Anna, a Lithuanian refugee she took in during the war, served as Rosemary's housekeeper for a time in exchange for her patronage. As for romance, though the papers teased she knew "too much about men to get married," she confessed to one great love affair, "still the one and only."

She married that one and only – Harry Myers – sometime in late 1924/early 1925, after he divorced childhood sweetheart Nellie Campbell. The two wed in 1907 and had three children together; Myers initiated proceedings, Nellie countered on charges of desertion, and won alimony plus full custody of Harry Jr, Nellie Mae, and Mary Pickford(!). Fan magazines were delirious that their old favorites were a couple, some saying they'd been "engaged" before he married Nellie. Since this would've been almost impossible – and I realize I'm speculating here – it seems like a polite attempt to define their earlier relationship together. By 1930 they were living in Los Angeles and in 1938, Rosemary and Harry Myers sign a petition requesting "career insurance" in California. It requested legislation deducting 10% of all actors' salary to be saved by the State Treasurer in a sort of pension for when they retire. Other signatures included Jean Acker, Alice Lake, Elinor Fair, and Gertrude Astor. Harry Myers died of pneumonia on Christmas Day 1938, after three days "in a hospital room paid for by the film industry's relief fund." He was 56. Obituaries listed Rosemary as his only survivor; none mentioned his children or ex-wife.

After Myers' death, Rosemary became the third wife of Truitt Hughes, an attorney, writer, lecturer, and real estate broker who ran for CA public office in the 1920s. He'd been previously married to Rosemary Baldwin after his first wife Helen's death in 1922. (Having two wives named "Rosemary Hughes" led to some frustrating research!) The couple lived in Carlsbad, CA, for a time, then moved to La Mesa by 1945. In retirement Rosemary would often talk of the old days, when they'd "all meet at the subway on our way to work, and talk, and laugh. We were just working people then . . . ."

CASE CLOSED

Rosemary Theby died at the Virgil Convalescent Hospital in Los Angeles on November 10, 1973, of "circulatory shock" brought on by emphysema and "myocardial insufficiency." Her remains were cremated and interred at Westwood Memorial Park. Rosemary was 81.

MUGSHOTS

Rosemary and Rose Coghlan in As You Like It *(1912). Photo courtesy the Media History Digital Library.*

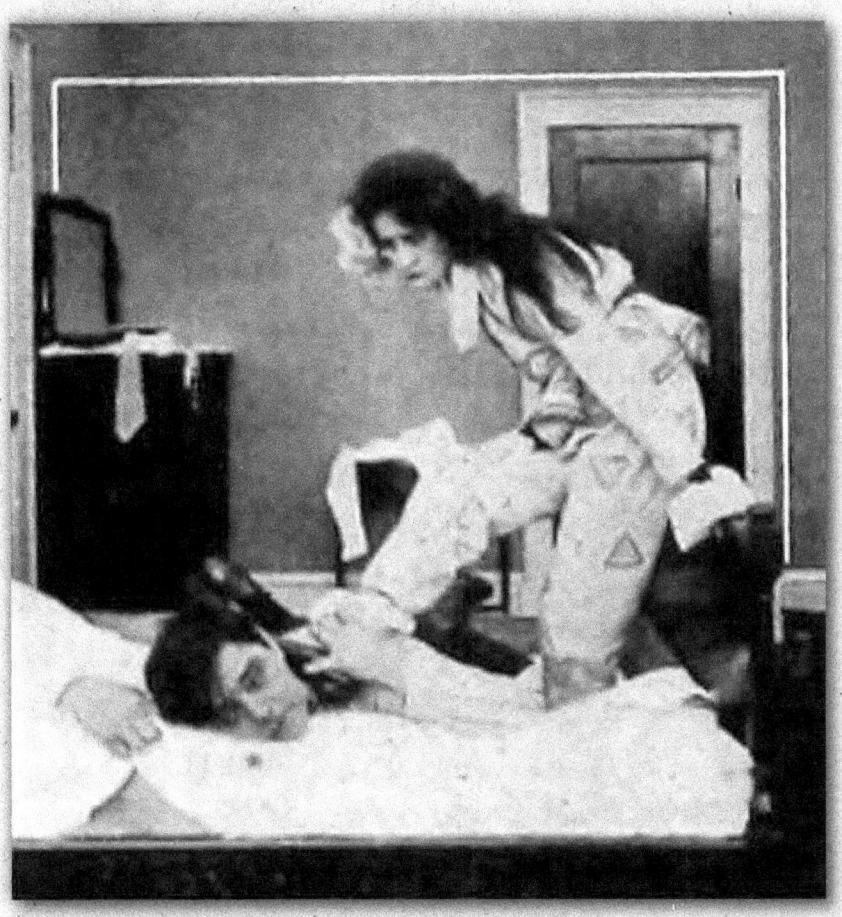
Scene from a Myers-Theby comedy. Photo courtesy the Media History Digital Library.

Rosemary in lace. Photo courtesy the Media History Digital Library.

Rosemary in 1921. Photo courtesy the Media History Digital Library.

Photo courtesy the Media History Digital Library.

FILE #49908: RUTH TAYLOR

REAL NAME: Ruth Alice Taylor
DOB: January 13, 1905 (some sources say 1908) – Grand Rapids, MI
HAIR: "as golden as a miner's dream"
EYES: "blue as the notes of a tenor sax" (with a little grey thrown in)
WANTED FOR: violation of the General Mining Act of 1872
ON THE RECORD: "You never can tell simply from conversation and compliments whether a man will yield a diamond tiara or merely an invitation to lunch."

BACKGROUND

Norman Taylor and his wife Ivah Bates had their only child Ruth in Michigan, and shortly after moved to Portland, OR. They lived with Ivah's mother Carrie while Norman worked in real estate, then managed a shoe store during Ruth's high school years. The family relocated to California after Ruth's graduation, and Ruth grabbed some extra work at Universal, Fox, and Warner Bros.

Mack Sennett put out a casting call in February 1925 for something specific: He was making a Harry Langdon short for Pathé and wanted "a blonde, vivacious, yet a sympathetic kind of girl . . . 'something like Alice Day'." Over a hundred young ladies tried out before Ruth won. Sennett signed her to a long-term contract not just for her "taffy-colored hair," but her personality. "Nine out of ten girls today look alike," he lamented. "[T]here was one – only one – who answered our requirements." Every newspaper's entertainment section praised the newcomer's "youth, refinement, beauty, vivacity, and natural talent."

MOVING PICTURES: SCHOOLS OF IMMORALITY

Ruth's first official screen appearance was in Sennett's *The Iron Nag* (Pathé, 1925), a horse racing comedy starring Billy Bevan. She did appear in the aforementioned Langdon short – *Lucky Stars* (1925), featuring Natalie Kingston – but her role was minor and uncredited. From 1925-1927, she made over 30 Sennett shorts, playing everything from maids to bathing beauties alongside Ben Turpin, Alice Day, and Raymond McKee. She teamed up for several with fellow "[up and] comer" Ralph Graves, and even got her own starring vehicle, *Dangerous Curves Behind* (1925), where she is wooed by Joseph Young (brother of Robert, later billed as Roger Moore – no, not 007). It was a comfortable, if predictable, living . . . until Lorelei came along.

Anita Loos' comically caustic 1925 novel *Gentlemen Prefer Blondes: The Intimate Diary of a Professional Lady* satirized social / sexual behavior of the upper class through the eyes of shrewd yet lovably dopey "kept" woman Lorelei Lee, and her acerbic best friend, Dorothy Shaw. Loos was inspired by an encounter between good friend H.L. Mencken and an attractive blonde who reduced him to jelly. The inimitable Loos wit made it an instant classic (it sold out upon release) and she, along with husband/ frequent collaborator John Emerson, adapted it into the hit 1926 Broadway play starring June Walker and Edna Hibbard.

The search for a screen Lorelei was bested only by the Scarlett O'Hara search ten years later. Every blonde in Hollywood – as many as there were "bootleggers to the block in Manhattan" – craved the role, and over 2000 swarmed initial casting calls. Suggestions abounded in fan magazines, among them Clara Bow, Esther Ralston, Sally Rand, Josephine Dunn, and Blanche Mehaffey, but Loos herself had final say. Finding Dorothy was easier: Louise Brooks had the "dark magnetic eyes [and] drawling smile". Stories differ as to how Ruth won the coveted role. One version said Loos exclaimed "That's Lorelei Lee!" after finding Ruth's photo in an old casting directory; another, more plausible version gave John Emerson the honors. Exhausted after a full day of tryouts, he went over to the "sixth blonde" and announced he was shutting things down for the day. Ruth, indignant after waiting nine hours, gave Emerson a piece of her mind and – "the moment I heard those pipes of hers I knew she was *Lorelei*." Ruth, nicknamed "The Little Girl with a Big Personality" at Sennett, mailed 14,000 photos of herself out via Paramount to celebrate the decision, and the rest of the cast was locked down by late 1927: Ford Sterling, Holmes Herbert, Mack Swain, Trixie Friganza, and Chester Conklin. Mal St. Clair was the director, and titles were co-written by Loos and Herman J. Mankiewicz. This was shaping up to be a real firecracker!

Gentlemen Prefer Blondes (Famous Players-Lasky/Paramount, 1928) opened to intense anticipation with one hiccup: Louise Brooks, for "unknown" reasons, was replaced by Alice White. (Rumor had it Brooksie all but stole the picture in early rushes.) Did it live up to the hype? Depends on whom you ask. Mordaunt Hall of the *New York Times* was charmed by Ruth's "big blue eyes" and her "clever" ability to make them "sparkle at the mere suggestion of precious stones . . . [t]his film is an infectious treat." *Motion Picture News* and *Variety* both felt something was lacking, the latter finding it "sapped up" for the public while conceding to "plenty of laughs for the wise girls [and] plenty of spots to wise up the girls who aren't." *Picture Play* called Ruth "excellent" in a role "barely escap[ing] monotony" but admitted it wasn't until Alice White's entrance that things "pick[ed] up enormously." Fans resented Ruth for taking the role from their "favorites" and gave her a chilly reception; one letter from Baltimore, MD read "I was keenly disappointed in the much-heralded Ruth Taylor ... if [she] ever reaches the heights, then I shall be much mistaken." Exhibitors, prepared for a blockbuster, suffered. "We believed the production's publicity and exploited it heavily," said one from Las Vegas, NV. "Just too bad. Could have been one of the real big ones and it is just ordinary." Paramount held back on further promotion for Ruth until they saw official box office receipts. In the meantime, she was voted a 1928 WAMPAS Baby Star (alongside Alice Day) and spent time with Madeline Hurlock at Arrowhead Springs, a health resort, where they sought diet advice on gaining weight. Costume designer Travis Banton allegedly loved how "tiny" Ruth was, finding the actress "a never-ending joy" to dress. When she returned, Paramount had plans for her.

Just Married (Paramount, 1928) was the inaugural comedy in the studio's new team of Ruth and James Hall, also featuring William Austin and Lila Lee. "Very light screen fare" about a tangle of engaged and jilted couples sorting themselves out into the proper matchups on board an ocean liner. It didn't make waves and effectively ended the proposed Taylor-Hall franchise. After a month-long bout with "intestinal influenza," Ruth signed on for two projects: an untitled one opposite Charles "Buddy" Rogers, and "Babs" in Clara Bow's first talkie *The Wild Party* (1929).

A Hint to Brides (Paramount, 1929): Newlyweds Ruth and Johnny Arthur come home to find a robbery in progress. Rather than call the cops, the bride hands the thief their duplicate wedding gifts. Only one problem: their new insurance policy doesn't cover burglary. "A fair amount of laughs," said *Film Daily* of the Christie comedy, with an "amusing" finale. *Variety* thought those laughs "widely spaced" and that Ruth "mugg[ed] excessively." This was Ruth's lackluster talkie debut; the Buddy Rogers project never materialized, and her role in *The Wild Party* (1929) went to Adrienne Doré.

The College Coquette (Columbia, 1929): Ruth is the campus flirt, involved in a love quadrangle with Buster Collier, Jobyna Ralston, and John Holland, in "just another college picture" written by old partner Ralph Graves. They already oversaturated the market; "a drunken party of university flaming and thirsty youths ... doesn't make the picture any better," complained *Variety*. *Screenland* called it "a story without merit" with "all the old ingredients." Critics not only snubbed Ruth's voice ("throaty and guttural") and performance ("overplayed," "flat") but mocked her career trajectory, "dear little collegiate Lorelei" who was "on the horizon for a brief moment." *Photoplay* pitied her and "her failure to live up to predictions," praying for a miracle before her star had "no direction to bow but out."

This Thing Called Love (Pathé, 1929): This comedy offered Edmund Lowe, Constance Bennett, a color ("not Technicolor but Multicolor") sequence, and a small part for Ruth as "Dolly." The plot: Man hires woman to act as his wife everywhere but the bedroom; they both maintain separate relationships, sparking unexpected jealousy; man and woman realize they actually love each other. Good reviews, "just as well or better" as the Edwin Burke play on which it was based. Ruth is not mentioned, other than *Photoplay* wondering "if she will ever be able to cash in fully on the break she got [in *Blondes*]."

Scrappily Married (Paramount, 1930): Ruth and Johnny Arthur reunite in another Christie two-reeler, this time about meek husbands, domineering wives, and a gift meant for one that ends up with the other. Bland, "general appeal" comedy with Bert Roach and Mabel Forrest. *Motion Picture News* advised exhibitors to "give it plenty of support. It needs it." This was Ruth Taylor's final film.

OTHER SORDID DETAILS

Ruth retired and married Paul Steinberg Zuckerman on March 17, 1930. Anita Loos joked that Ruth embodied Lorelei so thoroughly "that she married a multimillionaire and quit work!" Zuckerman was a successful stockbroker and highly decorated Air Force brigadier general who served in both World Wars. Their son, Henry, was born December 9, 1930.

Fan magazines mourned her, Hope Drown, Fay Lanphier, and Betty Bronson as Hollywood's "Cinderellas who failed to find the happy ending." *Film Daily* felt the box office might even "perk up a bit" if she returned to movies. Nothing doing: Ruth delighted in life on Manhattan's Park Avenue as wife, mother, and socialite, "interested only in wall paper [sic], draperies, and furniture." Henry went to military school, Paul was partner at Zuckerman, Smith & Co., and Ruth schmoozed at dinner parties with Sally Eilers, Stella Adler, and Mrs. Ricardo Cortez. (She also allegedly had her nose done.) Everyone liked her, from former fans who thought no one "more radiant [or] friendlier" to close friends Laura La Plante, Janet Gaynor, Mary Martin and Alice Faye who adored her "warmth and charm...honesty...bright mind [and] good conversation." Lauren Bacall and Humphrey Bogart chose her as godmother for their daughter Leslie.

Henry went to Choate like his father, then to Dartmouth. Taking a family nickname as his professional one, Buck Henry wrote and performed for Steve Allen and on "That Was the Week That Was." He co-created and wrote for TV's popular spy spoof "Get Smart," received two Oscar nominations (in 1968 for Best Adapted Screenplay for *The Graduate*, and in 1979 for Best Director for *Heaven Can Wait*), and frequently hosted "Saturday Night Live" from 1976-1980, often appearing in skits as recurring characters Howard, Uncle Roy, or Mr. Dantley – the last of which resulted in a minor head injury from Samurai Futaba (John Belushi)'s katana. A prolific TV guest star on everything from "Murphy Brown" to "30 Rock," he was most recently seen on TNT's "Franklin & Bash" in 2013.

Paul died in 1965 following an operation. Ruth, now living in Palm Springs, CA, threw everything into her home, creating a tropical oasis for entertaining complete with "outdoor gazebo and pool." And plants, lots of plants, which she called "miracle[s] . . . a magic something not to be taken lightly." Abundant flowers and paintings by Matisse and Andy Warhol enjoyed pride of place in her "desert hideaway," which local papers profiled several times. Ruth's other great love was animals, working with veterinarian Dr. Robert Lawson for several charities like "Animal Samaritans" and "Lend-A-Paw." She never lost that inner socialite, however, and as late as January 1984 threw a "Sunday night soiree" attended by Francis Lederer, Constance Moore, Diane "Mousie" Lewis Powell, and former Columbia head Leo Jaffe.

CASE CLOSED

Ruth Taylor died of natural causes in her home on April 12, 1984; one of her maids reportedly discovered her. She was cremated and interred at Desert Memorial Park in Cathedral City, CA. Ruth was 79 (76).

MUGSHOTS

Ruth, the girl of the hour. Photo courtesy the Media History Digital Library.

Ruth and Alice White in Gentlemen Prefer Blondes *(1928). Photo courtesy the Media History Digital Library.*

Ruth and James Hall. Photo courtesy the Media History Digital Library.

Exhibit A: Selected Bibliography

Initial Appearance

"Newark Police Judge Puts Lid on Vampires Who Flirt With Men." *Star-Gazette* (Elmira, NY), March 27, 1919.

Bean, Jennifer M. and Diane Negra, ed. (2002). *A Feminist Reader in Early Cinema (a Camera Obscura Book)*. Duke University Press.

Dijkstra, Bram (1996). *Evil Sisters: The Threat of Female Sexuality and the Cult of Manhood*. Knopf.

Haskell, Molly (1987). *From Reverence to Rape: The Treatment of Women in the Movies*. 2nd ed. University of Chicago Press.

Lee, Guy Carleton, *et. al.* "Literature - Types in Fiction: IV, the Adventuress." *The Sun* (Baltimore, MD), January 20, 1902.

Alice Hollister

"New York, New York City Marriage Records, 1829-1940," database, *FamilySearch* (https://familysearch.org/ark:/61903/1:1:249S-3ZT : 10 February 2018), George Hollister and Alice Berger, 01 Nov 1905; citing Marriage, Manhattan, New York, New York, United States, New York City Municipal Archives, New York; FHL microfilm 1,558,497.

"'The Dancers' Has Universal Appeal." *Exhibitors Trade Review*, January 31, 1925.

"Alice Hollister is Leading Woman in 'The Money Master'." *Moving Picture World*, February 5, 1921.

"Alice Hollister Stars in 'The Lotus Woman'." *Baltimore Sun*, July 23, 1916.

"Alice Hollister, First Vampire." *Moving Picture World*, June 24, 1916.

"Alice Hollister." *Silent Hollywood.com: The Silent Film Database*. Web. Accessed February 22, 2018. <https://silenthollywood.com/alicehollister.html>

"Blazing the Trail to Ireland: The Kalem Film Company." *Irish America*. Web. Accessed January 3, 2018. <https://irishamerica.com/2011/12/blazing-the-trail-to-ireland/>

"From the Manger to the Cross (1912): A Silent Film Review." *Movies Silently*. Web. Accessed January 3, 2018. < http://moviessilently.com/2017/06/18/from-the-manger-to-the-cross-1912-a-silent-film-review/>

"George K. Hollister, Sr." Obituary. *Los Angeles Times*, March 31, 1952.

"Milestones." Review. *Variety*, September 10, 1920.

"Miss Alice Hollister – A Kalem Favorite." *Kalem Kalendar*, February 19, 1912.

"News Items of the Kalem Companies." *Kalem Kalendar*, December 15, 1911.

"Stanhope Wheatcroft." *IMDb: The Internet Movie Database*. Web. Accessed February 20, 2018. <https://www.imdb.com/name/nm0923657/>

"The Alien." Review. *Moving Picture World*, May 24, 1919.

"The Forgotten Law." Review. *Film Daily*, October 22, 1922.

"The Shadow Stage: Married Flirts." Review. *Photoplay*, December 1924.

"The Theatres." *Daily Telegram* (Clarksburg, WV), August 31, 1914.

"The Vampire." *Kalem Kalendar*, October 1, 1913.

Alice H. Hollister, Year: *1930*; Census Place: *Beverly Hills, Los Angeles, California*; Page: *3B*; Enumeration District: *0833*; FHL microfilm: *2339859*. Ancestry.com. *1930 United States Federal Census* [database on-line]. Provo, UT, USA: Ancestry.com Operations Inc, 2002. Original data: United States of America, Bureau of the Census. *Fifteenth Census of the United States, 1930*. Washington, D.C.: National Archives and Records Administration, 1930. T626, 2,667 rolls.

Alice Hollister, Ancestry.com. *U.S., Social Security Death Index, 1935-2014* [database on-line]. Provo, UT, USA: Ancestry.com Operations Inc, 2014.

Alice Hollister, *FindAGrave*. Web. Accessed January 3, 2018 < https://www.findagrave.com/memorial/18344/alice-hollister>

Alice Hollister, Year: *1920*; Census Place: *Los Angeles Assembly District 63, Los Angeles, California*; Roll: *T625_106*; Page: *3A*; Enumeration District: *160*. Ancestry.com. *1920 United States Federal Census* [database on-line]. Provo, UT, USA: Ancestry.com Operations, Inc., 2010. Images reproduced by FamilySearch. Original data: Fourteenth Census of the United States, 1920. (NARA microfilm publication T625, 2076 rolls). Records of the Bureau of the Census, Record Group 29. National Archives, Washington, D.C. Note: Enumeration Districts 819-839 are on roll 323 (Chicago City).

Alice Hollister, Year: *1940*; Census Place: *Glendale, Los Angeles, California*; Roll: *m-t0627-00229*; Page: *14B*; Enumeration District: *19-169*. Ancestry.com. *1940 United States Federal Census* [database on-line]. Provo, UT, USA: Ancestry.com Operations, Inc., 2012. Original data: United States of America, Bureau of the Census. *Sixteenth Census of the United States, 1940*. Washington, D.C.: National Archives and Records Administration, 1940. T627, 4,643 rolls.

Alphonsia Berger, Year: *1880*; Census Place: *North Brookfield, Worcester, Massachusetts*; Roll: *566*; Page: *127D*; Enumeration District: *860*. Ancestry.com and The Church of Jesus Christ of Latter-day Saints. *1880 United States Federal Census*[database on-line]. Lehi, UT, USA: Ancestry.com Operations Inc, 2010. 1880 U.S. Census Index provided by The Church of Jesus Christ of Latter-day Saints © Copyright 1999 Intellectual Reserve, Inc. All rights reserved. Original data: Tenth Census of the United States, 1880. (NARA microfilm publication T9, 1,454 rolls). Records of the Bureau of the Census, Record Group 29. National Archives, Washington, D.C.

Alphonsine Berger, Year: *1900*; Census Place: *Worcester Ward 7, Worcester, Massachusetts*; Page: *8*; Enumeration District: *1769*; FHL microfilm: *1240697*. Ancestry.com. *1900 United States Federal Census* [database on-line]. Provo, UT, USA: Ancestry.com Operations Inc, 2004. Original data: United States of America, Bureau of the Census. *Twelfth Census of the United States, 1900*. Washington, D.C.: National Archives and Records Administration, 1900. T623, 1854 rolls.

Blaisdell, George. "Sid Olcott in Traveltalk." *Moving Picture World*, January 17, 1914.

"Alice Hollister Back After Long Absence." *Oakland Tribune* (CA), April 18, 1920.

Bowers, Q. David (1995). "Hollister, George K." *Thanhouser Films: An Encyclopedia and History*. Thanhouser Company Film Preservation, Inc. Web. Accessed January 3, 2018. <https://www.thanhouser.org/tcocd/Biography_Files/indeqrls_.htm>

Bush, W. Stephen. "From the Manger to the Cross." *Moving Picture World*, October 26, 1912.

Daly, Phil M. "Along the Rialto." *Film Daily*, May 13, 1930.

Dean, James W. "It Was More Than Publicity That Made Alice Popular." *Pittsburgh Press*, May 24, 1921.

Doris Devega, Ancestry.com. *California, Death Index, 1940-1997* [database on-line]. Provo, UT, USA: Ancestry.com Operations Inc, 2000.

Gaddis, Pearl. "Lovely Alice Hollister." *Photoplay*, ca. 1915-1916. Clipping provided by Terry Ann Smith.

Gaddis, Pearl. "Taking Tea with Alice Hollister." *Photoplay*, February 1915.

George F. Hollister, Year: *1910*; Census Place: *Bronx Assembly District 34, New York, New York*; Roll: *T624_1001*; Page: *2B*; Enumeration District: *1563*; FHL microfilm: *1375014*. Ancestry.com. *1910 United States Federal Census* [database on-line]. Lehi, UT, USA: Ancestry.com Operations Inc, 2006. Original data: Thirteenth Census of the United States, 1910 (NARA microfilm publication T624, 1,178 rolls). Records of the Bureau of the Census, Record Group 29. National Archives, Washington, D.C.

George K. Hollister, Ancestry.com. *California, Death Index, 1940-1997* [database on-line]. Provo, UT, USA: Ancestry.com Operations Inc, 2000.

Hall, Mordaunt. "The Screen." *New York Times*, November 19, 1924.

Hoffmann, Esther. "Famous Reel Vampires Tell Why They Wouldn't Be Real Vampires." *Salt Lake Telegram* (UT), April 11, 1915.

L.A. Yvonne Berger, Ancestry.com. *Massachusetts, Death Records, 1841–1915* [database on-line]. Provo, UT, USA: Ancestry.com Operations, Inc., 2013.

McGowan, John J. (2005). *J.P. McGowan: Biography of a Hollywood Pioneer.* McFarland.

Rosalie Allis [sic] Berger, Ancestry.com. *Massachusetts, Town and Vital Records, 1620-1988* [database on-line]. Provo, UT, USA: Ancestry.com Operations, Inc., 2011.

Sears, Elizabeth. "A Vampire Off Guard." *Film Fun*, September 1916.

Smith, Terry Ann (May 7, 2018.) Email interview with author.

Webster, H. Kent. "An Irish Classic in Three Reels." *Motography*, October 1911.

Carmen Phillips

"'Piff, Paff, Pouf' is Needed Tonic." *Los Angeles Herald*, June 23, 1909.

"2 Wreckers of Film Homes on Same Bill." *Los Angeles Herald*, February 20, 1917.

"A Small Estate." *Oakland Tribune* (CA), April 11, 1888.

"All Souls' Eve." Review. *Film Daily*, February 20, 1921.

"Carmen Collier Services Held." *Arcadia Tribune* (CA), December 18, 1966.

"Carmen is Favorite." *Los Angeles Times*, February 20, 1910.

"Celebrate Cast in Warner Production." *Billings Gazette* (MT), July 20, 1919.

"Fair Motorists Enjoy Fast Ride in National." *Los Angeles Herald*, July 10, 1910.

"Fair Week." Review. *Variety*, June 4, 1924.

"For A Woman's Honor." Review. *Motion Picture News*, September 27, 1919.

"Forbidden Paths." Review. *Photoplay*, October 1917.

"Hollywood." *AFI Catalog of Feature Films, The First 100 Years 1893-1993: American Film Institute.* Web. Accessed October 17, 2018. <http://catalog.afi.com/Catalog/MovieDetails/9785>

"Invalid's Home Fired by Tramps." *Oakland Tribune* (CA), December 28, 1915.

"Lady of Lourdes Academy: Graduation Exercises at Father Gleeson's School for Girl's [sic]." *Oakland Tribune* (CA), June 6, 1891.

"Love-Lorn Swain Goes on Rampage." *Oakland Tribune* (CA), October 12, 1909.

"Maria J. Phillips." Obituary. *Oakland Tribune* (CA), January 4, 1924.

"Mrs. Temple's Telegram." Review. *Film Daily*, May 16, 1920.

"Novelty." *Oakland Tribune* (CA), August 30, 1908.

"Oakland Girl is Clever Member Of 'Piff, Paff, Pouf' Company." *Oakland Tribune* (CA), June 14, 1909.

"One Dead; Hundred Hurt." *Los Angeles Times*, November 12, 1918.

"Picture Folk Injured." *Los Angeles Times*, November 13, 1918.

"Portugese Hold Big Celebration." *Oakland Tribune* (CA), October 6, 1916.

"Simply Adores Plane Sailing." *Los Angeles Times*, January 25, 1911.

"The Broadway." *Charlotte Observer* (NC), August 11, 1919.

"The Great Air Robbery." *AFI Catalog of Feature Films, The First 100 Years 1893-1993: American Film Institute.* Web. Accessed October 17, 2018. <http://catalog.afi.com/Catalog/MovieDetails/15618>
"The Great Air Robbery." Review. *Film Daily,* January 4, 1920.
"The Heart Specialist." *Moving Picture World,* April 1, 1922.
"The Home Town Girl." Review. *Billboard,* May 31, 1919.
"The Hope Diamond Mystery." *IMDb: The Internet Movie Database.* Web. Accessed October 13, 2018. < https://www.imdb.com/title/tt0012293/>
"The Screen." *Lebanon Daily News* (PA), February 17, 1921.
"Thirty Days." Review. *Exhibitors Trade Review,* December 23, 1922.
"William Collier." Obituary. *Independent Star-News* (Pasadena, CA), July 7, 1957.
"William Desmond, Strand Theater, in 'Whitewashed Walls,' Today." *San Bernardino Sun* (CA), April 27, 1919.
Advertisement for the Bristol Pier Café, *Los Angeles Herald,* July 30, 1910.
Anna Phillips, Year: *1900*; Census Place: *Oakland Ward 2, Alameda, California*; Page: *10*; Enumeration District: *0342*; FHL microfilm: *1240082.* Ancestry.com. *1900 United States Federal Census* [database on-line]. Provo, UT, USA: Ancestry.com Operations Inc, 2004. Original data: United States of America, Bureau of the Census. *Twelfth Census of the United States, 1900.* Washington, D.C.: National Archives and Records Administration, 1900. T623, 1854 rolls.
Campbell, Donna M. (2016). *Bitter Tastes: Literary Naturalism and Early Cinema in American Women's Writing.* University of Georgia Press.
Carmen K. Collier, Ancestry.com. *California, Death Index, 1940-1997* [database on-line]. Provo, UT, USA: Ancestry.com Operations Inc, 2000.
Certificate of Death: Carmen Katherine Collier. Filed December 14, 1966, State of California, County of Los Angeles, Dept. of Health, Reg. Dist. No. 7097-052613, State File No. (absent). Informant: Helen M. McGann [friend].
Colwell, Mosgrove. "Something New in Pictures." *Motion Picture,* September 1916.
Gifford, Denis (1973). *Karloff: The Man, the Monster, the Movies.* Curtis Books.
Katchmer, George. "Carmen Phillips." *Classic Images,* April 1994.
Manuel Phillips, Author: *California. Superior Court (Alameda County)*; Probate Place: *Alameda, California.* Ancestry.com. *California, Wills and Probate Records, 1850-1953* [database on-line]. Provo, UT, USA: Ancestry.com Operations, Inc., 2015.
Manuel Phillips, Year: *1880*; Census Place: *Oakland, Alameda, California*; Roll: *61*; Page: *84D*; Enumeration District: *005.* Ancestry.com and The Church of Jesus Christ of Latter-day Saints. *1880 United States Federal Census* [database on-line]. Lehi, UT, USA: Ancestry.com Operations Inc, 2010. 1880 U.S. Census Index provided by The Church of Jesus Christ of Latter-day Saints © Copyright 1999 Intellectual Reserve, Inc. All rights reserved. Original data: Tenth Census of the United States, 1880. (NARA microfilm publication T9, 1,454 rolls). Records of the Bureau of the Census, Record Group 29. National Archives, Washington, D.C.

Mary J. Phillips, Year: *1910*; Census Place: *Oakland Ward 2, Alameda, California*; Roll: *T624_70*; Page: *2A*; Enumeration District: *0087*; FHL microfilm: *1374083*. Ancestry.com. *1910 United States Federal Census* [database on-line]. Lehi, UT, USA: Ancestry.com Operations Inc, 2006. Original data: Thirteenth Census of the United States, 1910 (NARA microfilm publication T624, 1,178 rolls). Records of the Bureau of the Census, Record Group 29. National Archives, Washington, D.C.

Olympius, Shirley. "The Theaters." *Los Angeles Herald*, July 19, 1910.

Reid, John Howard (2011*). Silent Movies & Early Sound Films on DVD: New Expanded Edition*. Lulu.com.

William H. Collier, Year: *1940*; Census Place: *Los Angeles, Los Angeles, California*; Roll: *m-t0627-00407*; Page: *34A*; Enumeration District: *60-224*. Ancestry.com. *1940 United States Federal Census* [database on-line]. Provo, UT, USA: Ancestry.com Operations, Inc., 2012. Original data: United States of America, Bureau of the Census. *Sixteenth Census of the United States, 1940*. Washington, D.C.: National Archives and Records Administration, 1940. T627, 4,643 rolls.

William Handley Collier, Ancestry.com. *California, Death Index, 1940-1997* [database on-line]. Provo, UT, USA: Ancestry.com Operations Inc, 2000.

Wm. H. Collier, Ancestry.com. *U.S. City Directories, 1822-1995* [database on-line]. Provo, UT, USA: Ancestry.com Operations, Inc., 2011.

Claire de Lorez

"'The Queen of Sheba' a Lavish Production." *Exhibitors Herald*, April 30, 1921.

"'The Siren of Seville' is Acclaimed by N.Y. Critics." *Moving Picture World*, December 6 1924.

"'Under the Rouge' New Moomaw Title." *Motion Picture News*, May 23, 1925.

"A New Year's Change." *San Francisco Chronicle*, December 31, 1898.

"A Notable Opening." *San Francisco Call*, September 29, 1905.

"Actors Mourn Old Man Booze." *New York Clipper*, May 7, 1919.

"Actress Takes Lethal Poison." *Los Angeles Times*, September 27, 1932.

"Actress Who Inspired Glynn's [sic] 'It' Lies Dying." *Journal-Gazette* (Mattoon, IL), September 28, 1932.

"Beau Brummel." *AFI Catalog of Feature Films, The First 100 Years 1893-1993: American Film Institute*. Web. Accessed April 23, 2018. <http://catalog.afi.com/Catalog/MovieDetails/ 2764>

"Broadway by Walter Winchell." *Honolulu Advertiser* (HI), June 1, 1944.

"Claire De Lorez Injured in Crash." *Exhibitors Herald*, June 23, 1921.

"Claire de Lorez is Newest 'Rage'." *Ogden Standard-Examiner* (UT), October 15, 1924.

"Claire de Lorez Near to Death." *Davenport Democrat & Leader* (IA), October 5, 1924.

"Claire De Lorez to Wed." *Los Angeles Times*, June 3, 1924.

"Claire de Lorez." *Salt Lake Telegram* (UT), March 3, 1924.

"Enemies of Women." *AFI Catalog of Feature Films, The First 100 Years 1893-1993: American Film Institute*. Web. Accessed April 23, 2018. <http://catalog.afi.com/Catalog/MovieDetails/ 8840>

"Enemies of Women." Review. *Screen Opinions*, May 1-5, 1923.

"Father's Close Shave." Review. *Film Daily*, May 23, 1920.

"Four Horsemen of the Apocalypse." Review. *Variety*, February 18, 1921.

"Gives Hollywood the Ha-Ha." *Pittsburgh Press*, April 2, 1927.

"Hard to Match the Beauty of His Wife." *Baltimore Sun*, July 27, 1924.

"Her Night of Romance." *Visual Education*, December 1924.

"L'équipage 1928." *Ann Harding's Treasures*. Web. Accessed September 20, 2018. < http://annhardingstreasures.blogspot.com/2012/03/lequipage-1928.html>

"Morgane la Sirène 1927." *Ann Harding's Treasures*. Web. Accessed September 20, 2018. < http://annhardingstreasures.blogspot.com/2010/12/morgane-la-sirene-1927.html>

"Morgane." Review. *Variety*, June 26, 1929.

"Part III – Deutches and the Anniversary of the SFO Earthquake." *Vaporback Writer*. Web. Accessed January 10, 2018. < https://vaporbackwriter.wordpress.com/2010/04/17/part-iii-deutches-and-the-anniversary-of-the-sfo-earthquake/>

"Poisoned Star Fights for Life." *DuBois Courier-Express* (PA), September 28, 1932.

"So This is Marriage." *AFI Catalog of Feature Films, The First 100 Years 1893-1993: American Film Institute*. Web. Accessed April 23, 2018. <http://catalog.afi.com/Catalog/MovieDetails/12246>

"The Bright Lights of Broadway." Review. *Film Daily*, September 30, 1923.

"The Coast Patrol." Review. *Variety*, March 25, 1925.

"The Joyous Troublemakers." Review. *Moving Picture World*, July 10, 1920.

"The Net." Review. *Film Daily*, January 27, 1924.

"The Re-Creation of Brian Kent." Review. *Film Daily*, March 8, 1925.

"The Scuttlers." Review. *Film Daily*, December 19, 1920.

"The Siren of Seville." Review. *Theatrical Field*, February 1925.

"Thelma Deutch." *FindAGrave*. Web. Accessed August 3, 2018. <https://www.findagrave.com/memorial/107257491/thelma-d-deutch>

"Tourneur in Germany." *Variety*, August 15, 1928.

"Vittel." *Holocaust Encyclopedia: United States Holocaust Memorial Museum*. Web. Accessed January 10, 2018. <https://encyclopedia.ushmm.org/content/en/article/vittel>

Bell, Caroline. "Friendships Among the Screen Stars." *Picture-Play*, April 1925.

Benson, Sally. "The Screen in Review." *Picture-Play*, July 1925.

Blurb about "Cobra." *Muncie Evening Press* (IN), October 16, 1926.

Blurb about Claire, *Philadelphia Inquirer*, October 5, 1924.

Claire L. Deutch, Year: *1920*; Census Place: *San Francisco Assembly District 30, San Francisco, California*; Roll: *T625_139*; Page: *3B*; Enumeration District: *396*. Ancestry.com. *1920 United States Federal Census* [database on-line]. Provo, UT, USA: Ancestry.com Operations, Inc., 2010. Images reproduced by

FamilySearch. Original data: Fourteenth Census of the United States, 1920. (NARA microfilm publication T625, 2076 rolls). Records of the Bureau of the Census, Record Group 29. National Archives, Washington, D.C. Note: Enumeration Districts 819-839 are on roll 323 (Chicago City).

Claire L. Santel, Year: *1910*; Census Place: *San Francisco Assembly District 38, San Francisco, California*; Roll: *T624_99*; Page: *4A*; Enumeration District: *0181*; FHL microfilm: *1374112*. Ancestry.com. *1910 United States Federal Census* [database on-line]. Lehi, UT, USA: Ancestry.com Operations Inc, 2006. Original data: Thirteenth Census of the United States, 1910 (NARA microfilm publication T624, 1,178 rolls). Records of the Bureau of the Census, Record Group 29. National Archives, Washington, D.C.

Claire Typaldos-Bassia, Ancestry.com. *New York State, Passenger and Crew Lists, 1917-1967* [database on-line]. Provo, UT, USA: Ancestry.com Operations, Inc., 2008.

Edward J. Deutch, Ancestry.com. *Reports of Deaths of American Citizens Abroad, 1835-1974* [database on-line]. Provo, UT, USA: Ancestry.com Operations, Inc., 2010.

Edward J. Deutch, Year: *1920*; Census Place: *San Francisco Assembly District 33, San Francisco, California*; Roll: *T625_140*; Page: *17A*; Enumeration District: *262*. Ancestry.com. *1920 United States Federal Census* [database on-line]. Provo, UT, USA: Ancestry.com Operations, Inc., 2010. Images reproduced by FamilySearch. Original data: Fourteenth Census of the United States, 1920. (NARA microfilm publication T625, 2076 rolls). Records of the Bureau of the Census, Record Group 29. National Archives, Washington, D.C. Note: Enumeration Districts 819-839 are on roll 323 (Chicago City).

Hales, Barbara (editor), *et.al.* (2016). *Continuity and Crisis in German Cinema, 1928-1936 (Screen Cultures: German Film and the Visual)*. Camden House.

Jungmeyer, Jack. "Gossip of the Silver Screen." *The Town Talk* (Alexandria, LA), February 22, 1924.

Jungmeyer, Jack. "What's in a Name? Asks [sic] Latest Vamp." *Reading Times* (PA), May 24, 1924.

Kingsley, Grace. "Tea-Cup Tête-à-Tête with Stella, the Star-Gazer." *Los Angeles Times*, June 3, 1925.

Montrose M. Bernstein, Year: *1930*; Census Place: *Los Angeles, Los Angeles, California*; Page: *10A*; Enumeration District: *0196*; FHL microfilm: *2339875*. Ancestry.com. *1930 United States Federal Census* [database on-line]. Provo, UT, USA: Ancestry.com Operations Inc, 2002. Original data: United States of America, Bureau of the Census. *Fifteenth Census of the United States, 1930*. Washington, D.C.: National Archives and Records Administration, 1930. T626, 2,667 rolls.

Spain, Mildred. "Holdups, Fires and Murders, Gun Fights, Vamp – A Movie." *New York Daily News*, May 16, 1925.

Thelma Dolores Deutch, Ancestry.com. *California, San Francisco Area Funeral Home Records, 1895-1985* [database on-line]. Provo, UT, USA: Ancestry.com Operations, Inc., 2010.

De Sacia Mooers

"'Blonde Vampire's' Clothes Basis of Movie Suit." *New York Daily News*, November 1, 1921.

"Back to Liberty." Review. *Variety*, January 25, 1928.

"Blonde Vamp Lives." *Los Angeles Times*, September 26, 1920.

"Broadway Nights." Review. *Variety*, June 29, 1927.

"Bruenner and Persons Star Miss Mooers, Blond Vampire." *Moving Picture World*, August 28, 1920.

"By Whose Hand." Review. *Film Daily*, November 27, 1927.

"California Vamp Visits Son in School Here; Too Cold, He Goes Home." *Ithaca Journal* (NY), January 5, 1920.

"Can a Blonde Be a 'Vampire'?" *Oregon Daily Journal*, January 4, 1920.

"Cross Country Romance." *The Movies . . . 1940*, December 28, 1940.

"Dark Rosaleen." *IBDb: The Official Source for Broadway Information*. Web. Accessed September 25, 2018. < https://www.ibdb.com/broadway-production/dark-rosaleen-8867>

"De Sacia Mooers Lewis." Obituary. *Courier-News* (Bridgewater, NJ), January 12, 1960.

"De Sacia Mooers." *Motion Picture Almanac for 1931.*

"Edwin D. Mooers is Out of Jail." *Los Angeles Herald*, September 13, 1903.

"Farrel Spoils Pretty Romance." *Honolulu Advertiser* (HI), March 6, 1914.

"Finding Aid for the Harry L. Lewis and De Sacia Mooers papers (Collection 719) 1896-1954. UCLA Library Special Collections, Charles E. Young Research Library, UCLA." *Online Archive of California*. Web. Accessed May 3, 2018. < https://oac.cdlib.org/findaid/ark:/13030/kt1779p3b2/entire_text/>

"Forbidden Waters." Review. *Film Daily*, May 2, 1926.

"French Vamp Decries Tactics of Flapper." *Albany Daily Democrat* (NY), September 22, 1923.

"Gunning Has Ten New Pictures." *Motion Picture News*, March 11, 1922.

"How 'Vamps' are Used in Modern Business." *Courier-Journal* (Louisville, KY), August 5, 1923.

"Just Off Broadway." Review. *Film Daily*, February 10, 1929.

"Keith's – Last Half." *Dayton Daily News* (CA), February 5, 1928.

"Lonesome Ladies." *AFI Catalog of Feature Films, The First 100 Years 1893-1993: American Film Institute*. Web. Accessed May 7, 2018. <http://catalog.afi.com/Catalog/MovieDetails/10356>

"Marries the Girl; Challenged in Duel." *Spokane Press* (WA), April 5, 1910.

"Mrs. Victoria A. Saville." Obituary. *Los Angeles Times*, January 17, 1950.

"Pioneer Gets Rights to 'The Mystery Mind' Fifteen Episode Serial with All Star Cast." *Moving Picture World*, October 23, 1920.

"Potash and Perlmutter." *AFI Catalog of Feature Films, The First 100 Years 1893-1993: American Film Institute*. Web. Accessed May 7, 2018. <http://catalog.afi.com/Catalog/MovieDetails/1625>

"Potash and Perlmutter." Review. *Film Daily*, September 16, 1923.

"Secures State Artists to Support Cassinelli." *Motion Picture News*, May 31, 1919.
"Social Leader Seen in 'Forbidden Waters'." *Anaconda Standard* (MT), May 9, 1926.
"The Arizona Kid." *AFI Catalog of Feature Films, The First 100 Years 1893-1993: American Film Institute.* Web. Accessed May 7, 2018. <http://catalog.afi.com/Catalog/MovieDetails/1330>
"The Blonde Vampire." *AFI Catalog of Feature Films, The First 100 Years 1893-1993: American Film Institute.* Web. Accessed May 7, 2018. <http://catalog.afi.com/Catalog/MovieDetails/2917>
"The Blonde Vampire." Review. *Motion Picture News*, June 24, 1922.
"The Shadow Stage: Just Off Broadway." Review. *Photoplay*, April 1929.
"The Son of Tarzan." *ERBZine: The Official Edgar Rice Burroughs Tribute and Weekly Webzine Site.* Web. Accessed September 24, 2018. < http://www.erbzine.com/mag5/0589.html>
"Tongues of Scandal." Review. *Variety*, June 29, 2917.
"Wanted Career – Not Husband." *Healdsburg Tribune* (CA), May 29, 1925.
"Warbles No More." *Los Angeles Herald*, December 3, 1902.
"Will Please the Scotch." *Exhibitors Trade Review*, July 26, 1924.
Allan Leonard Rock, Ancestry.com. *New York, Naturalization Records, 1882-1944* [database on-line]. Provo, UT, USA: Ancestry.com Operations, Inc., 2012.
Blurb about "Dark Rosaleen," *Buffalo Enquirer* (NY), February 6, 1919.
Blurb about "Just Off Broadway," *Great Falls Tribune* (MT), November 3, 1929.
Blurb about "The Arizona Kid," *San Bernardino County Sun* (CA), June 8, 1930.
Blurb about Victor Connors, *Oakland Tribune* (CA), October 7, 1932.
Bone, James (2016). *The Curse of Beauty: The Scandalous & Tragic Life of Audrey Munson, America's First Supermodel.* Regan Arts.
Bystander, The. "Over the Teacups." *Photoplay*, October 1923.
DeLucia [sic] Mooers, Year: *1910*; Census Place: *Ballona, Los Angeles, California*; Roll: *T624_79*; Page: *14B*; Enumeration District: *0008*; FHL microfilm: *1374092*. Ancestry.com. *1910 United States Federal Census* [database on-line]. Lehi, UT, USA: Ancestry.com Operations Inc, 2006. Original data: Thirteenth Census of the United States, 1910 (NARA microfilm publication T624, 1,178 rolls). Records of the Bureau of the Census, Record Group 29. National Archives, Washington, D.C.
De Sacia M. Lewis, Ancestry.com. *California, Death Index, 1940-1997* [database on-line]. Provo, UT, USA: Ancestry.com Operations Inc, 2000.
De Sacia Mooers Lewis, *FindAGrave*. Web. Accessed January 23, 2018. < https://www.findagrave.com/memorial/118164074/de_sacia-lewis>
Douglas F. Mooers, *FindAGrave*. Web. Accessed May 7, 2018. < https://www.findagrave.com/memorial/118164091/douglas-f_-mooers>
Douglas Francis Mooers, Original data: State of California. *California Death Index, 1940-1997.* Sacramento, CA, USA: State of California Department of Health Services, Center for Health Statistics.

Edwin D. Mooers, Year: *1930*; Census Place: *Los Angeles, Los Angeles, California*; Page: *9B*; Enumeration District: *0360*; FHL microfilm: *2339881*. Ancestry.com. *1930 United States Federal Census* [database on-line]. Provo, UT, USA: Ancestry.com Operations Inc, 2002. Original data: United States of America, Bureau of the Census. *Fifteenth Census of the United States, 1930.* Washington, D.C.: National Archives and Records Administration, 1930. T626, 2,667 rolls.

Edwin Mooers, Ancestry.com. *New Jersey, Marriage Index, 1901-2016* [database on-line]. Lehi, UT, USA: Ancestry.com Operations, Inc., 2016.

Franc'Annie Saville, Ancestry.com. *Michigan, Births and Christenings Index, 1867-1911* [database on-line]. Provo, UT, USA: Ancestry.com Operations, Inc., 2011.

Frank Seville, Year: *1930*; Census Place: *San Francisco, San Francisco, California*; Page: *11B*; Enumeration District: *0401*; FHL microfilm: *2339945*. Ancestry.com. *1930 United States Federal Census* [database on-line]. Provo, UT, USA: Ancestry.com Operations Inc, 2002. Original data: United States of America, Bureau of the Census. *Fifteenth Census of the United States, 1930.* Washington, D.C.: National Archives and Records Administration, 1930. T626, 2,667 rolls.

Hall, Mordaunt. "Productions of Last Week." *New York Times*, May 25, 1930.

Lahue, Kalton C. (1968). *Bound and Gagged: The Story of the Silent Serials.* A.S. Barnes & Co., Inc.

Movie Weekly issues featuring the "Blonde-Brunette Vampire Contest":
- June 24, 1922
- July 22, 1922
- July 29, 1922
- August 12, 1922
- August 19, 1922

Ruby I. Tichenor, Year: *1940*; Census Place: *San Francisco, San Francisco, California*; Roll: *m-t0627-00303*; Page: *13A*; Enumeration District: *38-148*. Ancestry.com. *1940 United States Federal Census* [database on-line]. Provo, UT, USA: Ancestry.com Operations, Inc., 2012. Original data: United States of America, Bureau of the Census. *Sixteenth Census of the United States, 1940.* Washington, D.C.: National Archives and Records Administration, 1940. T627, 4,643 rolls.

Ruth Connors, Year: *1920*; Census Place: *San Francisco Assembly District 32, San Francisco, California*; Roll: *T625_138*; Page: *8B*; Enumeration District: *194*. Ancestry.com. *1920 United States Federal Census* [database on-line]. Provo, UT, USA: Ancestry.com Operations, Inc., 2010. Images reproduced by FamilySearch. Original data: Fourteenth Census of the United States, 1920. (NARA microfilm publication T625, 2076 rolls). Records of the Bureau of the Census, Record Group 29. National Archives, Washington, D.C. Note: Enumeration Districts 819-839 are on roll 323 (Chicago City).

Victoria Saville, Year: *1900*; Census Place: *San Francisco, San Francisco, California*; Page: *3*; Enumeration District: *0188*; FHL microfilm: *1240105*.

Ancestry.com. *1900 United States Federal Census* [database on-line]. Provo, UT, USA: Ancestry.com Operations Inc, 2004. Original data: United States of America, Bureau of the Census. *Twelfth Census of the United States, 1900.* Washington, D.C.: National Archives and Records Administration, 1900. T623, 1854 rolls.

Williams, Whitney. "Occupation – Housewife!" *Dayton Herald* (OH), August 8, 1934.

Edna Tichenor

"California, County Marriages, 1850-1952," database with images, *FamilySearch* (https://familysearch.org/ark:/61903/1:1:K8D3-Y3X : 8 December 2017), Joaquin Springer and Frances E Tichenor, 19 Jan 1918; citing , California, United States, county courthouses, California; FHL microfilm 2,050,856.

"'One Night in Rome' of Doubtful Value." *Exhibitors Trade Review*, November 15, 1924.

"Belasco Play Now Appearing As Film Is Well Worth While." *Santa Cruz Evening News* (CA), July 10, 1924.

"Black Moon." *AFI Catalog of Feature Films, The First 100 Years 1893-1993: American Film Institute.* Web. Accessed December 11, 2018. <http://catalog.afi.com/Catalog/MovieDetails/ 8498>

"Cast is Completed for 'Maytime' Film." *Baltimore Sun*, Sept 2, 1923.

"Drifting." *AFI Catalog of Feature Films, The First 100 Years 1893-1993: American Film Institute.* Web. Accessed December 11, 2018. <http://catalog.afi.com/Catalog/MovieDetails/ 8760>

"Edna Tichenor In It." *Los Angeles Times*, September 9, 1931.

"Edna Tichenor." *Classic Horror Film Board.* Web. Accessed December 14, 2017. < https://www.tapatalk.com/groups/monsterkidclassichorrorforum/edna-tichenor-t2201.html>

"Gold Diggers to Open At Temple on Sunday." *San Bernardino Sun* (CA), January 11, 1924.

"London After Midnight." *AFI Catalog of Feature Films, The First 100 Years 1893-1993: American Film Institute.* Web. Accessed December 11, 2018. <http://catalog.afi.com/Catalog/MovieDetails/10334>

"Maytime." Review. *Film Daily,* December 2, 1923.

"Nagel to Play Lead in Chaney Film." *Motion Picture News*, August 5, 1927.

"New Picture 'Find'." *San Francisco Examiner,* July 24, 1927.

"Noted Film Dog Dies." *Moving Picture World*, June 26, 1926.

"Officer of the Day." Review. *Motion Picture News*, February 13, 1926.

"The Gold Diggers." Review. *Motion Picture News*, September 22, 1923.

"The Gosh Darn Mortgage." Review. *Film Daily*, December 27, 1925.

"The Merry Widow." *AFI Catalog of Feature Films, The First 100 Years 1893-1993: American Film Institute.* Web. Accessed December 11, 2018. <http://catalog.afi.com/Catalog/MovieDetails/10733>

"The Show." Review. *Film Daily*, March 20, 1927.

"The Silent Accuser." Review. *Film Daily*, November 9, 1924.
"They Graduated into Pictures." *Los Angeles Times*, December 3, 1924.
Certificate of Death: Frances West. Filed November 19, 1965, State of California, County of Los Angeles, Dept. of Health, Reg. Dist. No. 7053-48832, State File No. (absent). Informant: Henry West [spouse].
Crown, Dave. "Reel Facts About Hollywood." *Petaluma Argus-Courier* (CA), August 29, 1936.
Edna F. Springer, Year: *1920*; Census Place: *Los Angeles Assembly District 72, Los Angeles, California*; Roll: *T625_113*; Page: *2A*; Enumeration District: *371*. Ancestry.com. *1920 United States Federal Census* [database on-line]. Provo, UT, USA: Ancestry.com Operations, Inc., 2010. Images reproduced by FamilySearch. Original data: Fourteenth Census of the United States, 1920. (NARA microfilm publication T625, 2076 rolls). Records of the Bureau of the Census, Record Group 29. National Archives, Washington, D.C. Note: Enumeration Districts 819-839 are on roll 323 (Chicago City).
Edna F. Tichenor, Year: *1910*; Census Place: *Los Angeles Assembly District 70, Los Angeles, California*; Roll: *T624_80*; Page: *3A*; Enumeration District: *0234*; FHL microfilm: *1374093*. Ancestry.com. *1910 United States Federal Census* [database on-line]. Lehi, UT, USA: Ancestry.com Operations Inc, 2006. Original data: Thirteenth Census of the United States, 1910 (NARA microfilm publication T624, 1,178 rolls). Records of the Bureau of the Census, Record Group 29. National Archives, Washington, D.C.
Edna Francis [sic] Tichenor, Ancestry.com. *Minnesota, Births and Christenings Index, 1840-1980* [database on-line]. Provo, UT, USA: Ancestry.com Operations, Inc., 2011.
Edna Tichenor, Year: *1930*; Census Place: *Los Angeles, Los Angeles, California*; Page: *2A*; Enumeration District: *0092*; FHL microfilm: *2339870*. Ancestry.com. *1930 United States Federal Census* [database on-line]. Provo, UT, USA: Ancestry.com Operations Inc, 2002. Original data: United States of America, Bureau of the Census. *Fifteenth Census of the United States, 1930.* Washington, D.C.: National Archives and Records Administration, 1930. T626, 2,667 rolls.
Frances Duzan, Ancestry.com. *California, County Birth, Marriage, and Death Records, 1849-1980* [database on-line]. Lehi, UT, USA: Ancestry.com Operations, Inc., 2017.
Frances Duzan, Year: *1940*; Census Place: *Los Angeles, Los Angeles, California*; Roll: *m-t0627-00398*; Page: *7B*; Enumeration District: *60-131*. Ancestry.com. *1940 United States Federal Census* [database on-line]. Provo, UT, USA: Ancestry.com Operations, Inc., 2012. Original data: United States of America, Bureau of the Census. *Sixteenth Census of the United States, 1940.* Washington, D.C.: National Archives and Records Administration, 1940. T627, 4,643 rolls.
Frances West, Ancestry.com. *California, Death Index, 1940-1997* [database on-line]. Provo, UT, USA: Ancestry.com Operations Inc, 2000. Original data: State of California. *California Death Index, 1940-1997.* Sacramento,

CA, USA: State of California Department of Health Services, Center for Health Statistics.

Goldbeck, Willis. "Facing Facts." *Motion Picture*, July 1922.

Hall, Mordaunt. "West of Zanzibar." Review. *New York Times*, December 31, 1928.

Hattie L. Tichenor, Ancestry.com. *California, Death Index, 1940-1997* [database on-line]. Provo, UT, USA: Ancestry.com Operations Inc, 2000.

Henry West, Ancestry.com. *U.S., Social Security Death Index, 1935-2014* [database on-line]. Provo, UT, USA: Ancestry.com Operations Inc, 2014.

Ira C. Tichenor, Year: *1920*; Census Place: *Salt Lake City Ward 5, Salt Lake, Utah*; Roll: *T625_1867*; Page: *9A*; Enumeration District: *164*. Ancestry.com. *1920 United States Federal Census* [database on-line]. Provo, UT, USA: Ancestry.com Operations, Inc., 2010. Images reproduced by FamilySearch. Original data: Fourteenth Census of the United States, 1920. (NARA microfilm publication T625, 2076 rolls). Records of the Bureau of the Census, Record Group 29. National Archives, Washington, D.C Note: Enumeration Districts 819-839 are on roll 323 (Chicago City).

Robert Joaquin Springer, Ancestry.com. *California, Death Index, 1940-1997* [database on-line]. Provo, UT, USA: Ancestry.com Operations Inc, 2000.

Skal, David J. and Elias Savada (1995). *Dark Carnival: The Secret World of Tod Browning*. Anchor Books/Doubleday.

Soister, John T. (2010). *Up from the Vault: Rare Thrillers of the 1920s and 1930s*. McFarland.

Walker, Brent E. (2009). *Mack Sennett's Fun Factory: A History and Filmography of His Studio and His Keystone and Mack Sennett Comedies, with Biographies of Players and Personnel, Vols. 1 & 2*. McFarland.

Iva Shepard

"Massachusetts State Vital Records, 1841-1920," database with images, *FamilySearch* (https://familysearch.org/ark:/61903/1:1:23YV-VQ3 : 15 October 2017), Lyle Chilson Clement and Iva Shafer Girton, 02 Feb 1918; citing Marriage, Fitchburg, Worcester, Massachusetts, United States, certificate number 31, page 342, State Archives, Boston.

"Answer Department." *Motion Picture*, December 1916.

"Correspondence." *San Francisco Dramatic Review*, August 28, 1909.

"Don Juan and the Starlets." *Ultimate I Love Lucy Wiki*. Web. Accessed April 26, 2018. <https://ultimateilovelucy.fandom.com/wiki/Ultimate_I_Love_Lucy_Wiki>

"In Slavery Days." Review. *Moving Picture World*, May 10, 1913.

"Iva Shepard in Gaumont Stock." *Moving Picture World*, May 6, 1916.

"Iva Shepard." *FindAGrave*. Web. Accessed January 19, 2018. <https://www.findagrave.com/memorial/9110141/iva-shepard>

"Ivy [sic] Shepard to Succeed Neva West in Girton Co." *Los Angeles Times*, July 28, 1910.

"Nursery School." *Ultimate I Love Lucy Wiki.* Web. Accessed April 26, 2018. <https://ultimateilovelucy.fandom.com/wiki/Ultimate_I_Love_Lucy_Wiki>
"Spotlights." *San Francisco Dramatic Review,* April 17, 1909.
"The Coquette." Review. *Moving Picture World,* November 18, 1911.
"The Drifter." Review. *Motography,* February 12, 1916.
"The Haunted Manor." *AFI Catalog of Feature Films, The First 100 Years 1893-1993: American Film Institute.* Web. Accessed April 23, 2018. <http://catalog.afi.com/Catalog/MovieDetails/14120>
"The Haunted Manor." Review. *Motion Picture News,* April 8, 1916.
"The Straight Road." Review. *Variety,* November 14, 1914.
"The Street of Seven Stars." Review. *Variety,* May 24, 1918.
"The Wife of Marcius." *Film Index,* April 2, 1910.
"Who's Who and Where." *Film Fun,* May 1916.
"Wilkes Players Form Independent Company." *Salt Lake Telegram* (UT), January 26, 1922.
Bernique, Jean (1916). *Motion Picture Acting for Professionals and Amateurs.* Producers Service Company.
Blurb about Iva Shepard, *Cincinnati Enquirer,* May 20, 1915.
Blurb in society column about Iva and Pearl, *News-Journal* (Mansfield, OH), January 16, 1909.
Bucci, Linda (May 2, 2018). Email interview with author.
Caward, Neil J. "Screen Gossip." *Picture Play,* June 1916.
Certificate of Death: Iva Shepard. Filed January 26, 1973, State of California, County of Los Angeles, Dept. of Health, Reg. Dist. No. 7097-004487, State File No. (absent). Informant: Iva Heaton [niece].
Chas Yorba, Ancestry.com. *California, County Birth, Marriage, and Death Records, 1849-1980* [database on-line]. Lehi, UT, USA: Ancestry.com Operations, Inc., 2017.
Chira. "The Science of the Hand." *Motion Picture,* May 1916.
Iva B. Shepard, Year: *1940*; Census Place: *Venice, Los Angeles, California*; Roll: *m-t0627-00258*; Page: *4A*; Enumeration District: *19-802B*. Ancestry.com. *1940 United States Federal Census* [database on-line]. Provo, UT, USA: Ancestry.com Operations, Inc., 2012. Original data: United States of America, Bureau of the Census. *Sixteenth Census of the United States, 1940.* Washington, D.C.: National Archives and Records Administration, 1940. T627, 4,643 rolls.
Iva Clements, Year: *1930*; Census Place: *Venice, Los Angeles, California*; Page: *6B*; Enumeration District: *1536*; FHL microfilm: *2339911*. Ancestry.com. *1930 United States Federal Census* [database on-line]. Provo, UT, USA: Ancestry.com Operations Inc, 2002. Original data: United States of America, Bureau of the Census. *Fifteenth Census of the United States, 1930.* Washington, D.C.: National Archives and Records Administration, 1930. T626, 2,667 rolls.
Iva Shafer, New York State Archives; Albany, New York; *State Population Census Schedules, 1915*; Election District: *37*; Assembly District: *21*; City: *New York*; County: *New York*; Page: *03*. Ancestry.com. *New York, State Census,*

1915 [database on-line]. Provo, UT, USA: Ancestry.com Operations, Inc., 2012. Original data: *State population census schedules, 1915.* New York State Archives, Albany, New York.

Iva Shafer, Year: *1900*; Census Place: *Chicago Ward 31, Cook, Illinois*; Page: *8*; Enumeration District: *0959*; FHL microfilm: *1240284*. Ancestry.com. *1900 United States Federal Census* [database on-line]. Provo, UT, USA: Ancestry.com Operations Inc, 2004. Original data: United States of America, Bureau of the Census. *Twelfth Census of the United States, 1900.* Washington, D.C.: National Archives and Records Administration, 1900. T623, 1854 rolls.

Kingsley, Grace. "Gold Diggers' Clever." *Los Angeles Times*, September 24, 1923.

Pearl R. Canfield, Ancestry.com. *California, Death Index, 1940-1997* [database on-line]. Provo, UT, USA: Ancestry.com Operations Inc, 2000. Original data: State of California. *California Death Index, 1940-1997*. Sacramento, CA, USA: State of California Department of Health Services, Center for Health Statistics.

Pearl R. Shafer, Ancestry.com. *Arizona, County Marriage Records, 1865-1972* [database on-line]. Lehi, UT, USA: Ancestry.com Operations, Inc., 2016.

Perry E. Girton, Ancestry.com. *Washington, Marriage Records, 1854-2013* [database on-line]. Provo, UT, USA: Ancestry.com Operations, Inc., 2012.

von Blon, Katherine. "Leatrice Joy Stars in 'Life With Mother'." *Los Angeles Times,* June 10, 1952.

Marcia Manon

"All's Fair in Love." Review. *Exhibitors Trade Review*, December 24, 1921.

"Ideal Cast Selected by Readers." *Motion Picture*, September 16, 1922.

"Joseph LaFrame [sic] Frothingham." *FindAGrave.* Web. Accessed January 16, 2018. < https://www.findagrave.com/memorial/6419679/joseph-laframe-frothingham>

"Marcia Manon Comes Back." *Los Angeles Times*, March 2, 1928.

"Marcia Manon, Film Actress, is Bride of Studio Manager." *Los Angeles Herald*, September 27, 1919.

"Old Wives for New." Review. *Variety*, May 24, 1918.

"One More American." Review. *Moving Picture World*, March 2, 1918.

"Signs New Star." *Los Angeles Times*, April 14, 1923.

"Stella Maris." *AFI Catalog of Feature Films, The First 100 Years 1893-1993:* American Film Institute. Web. Accessed April 23, 2018. <http://catalog.afi.com/Catalog/MovieDetails/17254>

"Stella Maris." *Paramount Press Book Collection, Vol 3: January 1918; Index Number 7.* Web. Accessed January 16, 2018. < https://archive.org/details/paramountpressbo03unse/page/n209>

"Stella Maris." Review. *Variety*, January 25, 1918.

"Talented Marcia Manon in Barrymore Support." *Moving Picture World*, February 15, 1919.

"The Hostage." Review. *Variety,* September 14, 1917.
"The Prison Without Walls." Review. *Variety,* April 27, 1917.
"The Test of Honor." Review. *Film Daily,* April 13, 1919.
"The Thing That Counts." *Chicago Tribune,* March 24, 1918.
"Truck, Train Crash Kills AV Woman." *San Bernardino County Sun* (CA), November 13, 1969.
Blurb about Julian's art, *Los Angeles Times,* August 11, 1929.
Blurb about Marcia, *Winnipeg Tribune* (Manitoba, Canada), March 15, 1930.
Blurb about name change, *Lincoln Star* (NE), January 13, 1918.
Certificate of Death: Marcia H. Frothingham (a.k.a. Marcia Manon, a.k.a. Elizabeth Frothingham). Filed April 12, 1973, State of California, County of San Bernardino, Dept. of Health, Reg. Dist. No. 8600-1868, State File No. (absent). Informant: Preneed Records/Deceased, Miss Marcia Manon, Victorville, Calif.
Cheatham, Maude. "Wanted: A Smile." *Motion Picture Classic,* May 1921.
Cornellia [sic] J. Harrison, Year: *1930*; Census Place: *Burbank, Los Angeles, California*; Page: *4B*; Enumeration District: *0850*; FHL microfilm: *2339860*. Ancestry.com. *1930 United States Federal Census* [database on-line]. Provo, UT, USA: Ancestry.com Operations Inc, 2002. Original data: United States of America, Bureau of the Census. *Fifteenth Census of the United States, 1930.* Washington, D.C.: National Archives and Records Administration, 1930. T626, 2,667 rolls.
Dan'l H Kathan, Ancestry.com. *California, County Birth, Marriage, and Death Records, 1849-1980* [database on-line]. Lehi, UT, USA: Ancestry.com Operations, Inc., 2017.
Daniel H. Kathan, Ancestry.com. *U.S. City Directories, 1822-1995* [database on-line]. Provo, UT, USA: Ancestry.com Operations, Inc., 2011.
Elizabeth H. Frothingham, Year: *1920*; Census Place: *Los Angeles Assembly District 63, Los Angeles, California*; Roll: *T625_106*; Page: *7A*; Enumeration District: *163*. Ancestry.com. *1920 United States Federal Census* [database on-line]. Provo, UT, USA: Ancestry.com Operations, Inc., 2010. Images reproduced by FamilySearch. Original data: Fourteenth Census of the United States, 1920. (NARA microfilm publication T625, 2076 rolls). Records of the Bureau of the Census, Record Group 29. National Archives, Washington, D.C. Note: Enumeration Districts 819-839 are on roll 323 (Chicago City).
Elizabeth Harrison, Year: *1940*; Census Place: *Los Angeles, Los Angeles, California*; Roll: *m-t0627-00403*; Page: *16A*; Enumeration District: *60-839*. Ancestry.com. *1940 United States Federal Census* [database on-line]. Provo, UT, USA: Ancestry.com Operations, Inc., 2012. Original data: United States of America, Bureau of the Census. *Sixteenth Census of the United States, 1940.* Washington, D.C.: National Archives and Records Administration, 1940. T627, 4,643 rolls.
Gifford, Denis (1973). *Karloff: The Man, the Monster, the Movies.* Curtis Books.

Joseph L. Frothingham, Ancestry.com. *California, County Birth, Marriage, and Death Records, 1849-1980* [database on-line]. Lehi, UT, USA: Ancestry.com Operations, Inc., 2017.

Joseph Laforme Frothingham, *"U.S., School Yearbooks, 1880-2012"*; Yearbook Title: *Harvard College Class of 1902 25th Anniversary Report*; Year: *1927*. Ancestry.com. U.S., School Yearbooks, 1900-1990 [database on-line]. Provo, UT, USA: Ancestry.com Operations, Inc., 2010.

Julian Harrison, Year: *1920*; Census Place: *Los Angeles Assembly District 63, Los Angeles, California*; Roll: *T625_106*; Page: *5A*; Enumeration District: *157*. Ancestry.com. *1920 United States Federal Census* [database on-line]. Provo, UT, USA: Ancestry.com Operations, Inc., 2010. Images reproduced by FamilySearch. Original data: Fourteenth Census of the United States, 1920. (NARA microfilm publication T625, 2076 rolls). Records of the Bureau of the Census, Record Group 29. National Archives, Washington, D.C. Note: Enumeration Districts 819-839 are on roll 323 (Chicago City).

Marcia H. Frothingham, Ancestry.com. *California, Death Index, 1940-1997* [database on-line]. Provo, UT, USA: Ancestry.com Operations Inc, 2000.

Mistley, Media. "Marcia Manon, Film Sphinx." *Motion Picture*, December 1918.

Naylor, Hazel Simpson. "Across the Silversheet." *Motion Picture*, June 1918.

Smith, Frederick James. "A Dreamer of Dreams." *Motion Picture Classic*, May 1919.

Wallace B. Harrison, Ancestry.com. *California, Death Index, 1905-1939* [database on-line]. Provo, UT, USA: Ancestry.com Operations, Inc., 2013.

Olga Grey

"A Vamp with a Goulash Name." *Picture-Play*, February 1917.

"Actor's 2d Will Filed." *New York Times*, September 29, 1953.

"Actress Admitted to California Bar." *Nevada State Journal*, December 10, 1932.

"Aged Mother Who Killed Own Son Gets Life Term." *Press Democrat* (Santa Rosa, CA), April 28, 1936.

"Egan Thespians Open Many Eyes At Recital." *Los Angeles Herald*, June 24, 1910.

"Ex-Actress in Court as Defendant." *Los Angeles Times*, April 10, 1930.

"Film Favorite Bares Secret Marriage." *Los Angeles Herald*, April 13, 1921.

"His Lesson." Review. *Moving Picture World*, January 16, 1915.

"Howard's Home: 211 Muirfield Road." *The Legendary Howard Hughes Jr.* Web. Accessed March 19, 2018. < https://hrhughesjr.webs.com/howardshome.htm>

"In Answer to Yours – ." *Photo-Play Journal*, June 1916.

"Inquiry in Actor's Death." *New York Times*, September 14, 1953.

"Intolerance." *AFI Catalog of Feature Films, The First 100 Years 1893-1993: American Film Institute.* Web. Accessed December 17, 2018. <http://catalog.afi.com/Catalog/MovieDetails/16253>

"Jim Bludso." *New York Clipper*, February 14, 1917.

"Legal Battle Looms Over Weber Millions." *New York Times*, September 26, 1953.
"Mary Garden to See It." *Los Angeles Times*, April 5, 1921.
"Million Dollar Will: 50-G Windfall to Queens Pal." *Long Island Star-Journal* (NY), April 9, 1955.
"Notorious Los Angeles Trials of the 20th Century: Sleepy Lagoon Murder and the Zoot Suit Riots." *L.A. Law Library*. Web. Accessed June 4, 2018. <http://www.lalawlibrary.org/pdfs/grants/Sleepy_Lagoon_Murder.pdf>
"Olga Gray Teaches Triangle Kiddies." *Statesman Journal* (Salem, OR), March 11, 1917.
"Olga Gray's Mother on Trial in Los Angeles Court." *Oakland Tribune* (CA), October 28, 1921.
"Olga Grey, Leads, Griffith Fine Arts." *Motion Picture News*, January 29, 1916.
"Pedro J. Gonzalez, 99, Folk Hero And Advocate for Social Justice." *New York Times*, March 24, 1995.
"Pickups by the Staff." *Camera!* December 4, 1920.
"Sisters in Tears As They Are Freed." *Los Angeles Herald*, October 27, 1921.
"Stefan Zacsek Jr." Obituary. *Los Angeles Times*, September 19, 1919.
"The Absentee." *AFI Catalog of Feature Films, The First 100 Years 1893-1993: American Film Institute*. Web. Accessed December 17, 2018. <http://catalog.afi.com/Catalog/MovieDetails/13733>
"The Birth of a Nation: Full Cast & Crew." *IMDb: The Internet Movie Database*. Web. Accessed December 17, 2018. < https://www.imdb.com/title/tt0004972/fullcredits?ref_=tt_cl_sm#cast>
"The Girl at Home." Review. *Variety*, May 4, 1917.
"The Lyric Stock Has Become a Very Popular Part of Portland Theatrical Life." *San Francisco Dramatic Review*, April 9, 1910.
"The Third Eye." Review. *Film Daily*, May 16, 1920.
"The Transformation of Olga Grey." *Curtains: Keeping early and silent film alive*. Web. Accessed January 15, 2018. < http://earlysilentfilm.blogspot.com/2013/04/the-transformation-of-olga-grey.html>
"The Woman God Forgot." Review. *Variety*, November 2, 1917.
"Trial Stops Old Feud of Two Sisters." *Los Angeles Times*, October 26, 1921.
"Triangle's Weekly Schedule." *Moving Picture World*, December 15, 1917.
"Two Sisters Held As 'Fence' Suspects." *Los Angeles Times*, July 16, 1921.
"Woman in Court As Receiver of Stolen Jewelry." *Los Angeles Herald*, July 7, 1921.
Anna Z. Weber, Ancestry.com. *Florida, Passenger Lists, 1898-1963* [database on-line]. Lehi, UT, USA: Ancestry.com Operations, Inc., 2006.
Anna Zacsek, Ancestry.com. *California, Federal Naturalization Records, 1843-1999* [database on-line]. Provo, UT, USA: Ancestry.com Operations, Inc., 2014.
Anna Zacsek, Ancestry.com. *California, Marriage Index, 1960-1985* [database on-line]. Provo, UT, USA: Ancestry.com Operations Inc, 2007.

Anna Zaecak [sic], Year: *1920*; Census Place: *Los Angeles Assembly District 64, Los Angeles, California*; Roll: *T625_108*; Page: *1B*; Enumeration District: *226*. Ancestry.com. *1920 United States Federal Census* [database on-line]. Provo, UT, USA: Ancestry.com Operations, Inc., 2010. Images reproduced by FamilySearch. Original data: Fourteenth Census of the United States, 1920. (NARA microfilm publication T625, 2076 rolls). Records of the Bureau of the Census, Record Group 29. National Archives, Washington, D.C. Note: Enumeration Districts 819-839 are on roll 323 (Chicago City).

Anna Zasek [sic], Year: *1900*; Census Place: *Manhattan, New York, New York*; Page: *15*; Enumeration District: *0794*; FHL microfilm: *1241116*. Ancestry.com. *1900 United States Federal Census* [database on-line]. Provo, UT, USA: Ancestry.com Operations Inc, 2004. Original data: United States of America, Bureau of the Census. *Twelfth Census of the United States, 1900.* Washington, D.C.: National Archives and Records Administration, 1900. T623, 1854 rolls.

Arnold Ray Samberg, Ancestry.com. *California, County Birth, Marriage, and Death Records, 1849-1980* [database on-line]. Lehi, UT, USA: Ancestry.com Operations, Inc., 2017.

Blurb about Zacsek and Orlando Weber Jr., *Honolulu Star Bulletin* (HI), December 4, 1946.

Carroll, Harrison. "Behind the Scenes in Hollywood." *The Times* (San Mateo, CA), May 29, 1936.

Certificate of Death: Anna Z. Windsor. Filed April 25, 1973, State of California, County of Los Angeles, Dept. of Health, Reg. Dist. No. 7097-017619, State File No. (absent). Informant: Stephen Windsor [spouse].

Crosse, John. "R. M. Schindler, Edward Weston, Margrethe Mather, Anna Zacsek, Lloyd Wright, Lawrence Tibbett, Reginald Pole, Beatrice Wood and Their Dramatic Circles." *Southern California Architectural History*. Web. Accessed January 15, 2018. < https://socalarchhistory.blogspot.com/2012/11/r-m-schindler-edward-weston-margrethe.html>

Fred. "Macbeth." Review. *Variety*, June 9, 1916.

Grey, Olga. "How I Learnt [sic] to Act." *Motion Picture*, December 1916.

Harrison, Louis Reeves. "Double Trouble." Review. *Moving Picture World*, November 13, 1915.

Haulman, Daniel L. "Safe Haven I and II." *Air Mobility Command Museum*. Web. Accessed March 28, 2018. < https://amcmuseum.org/history/safe-haven-i-and-ii/>

Istvan Kopcso, Ancestry.com. *New Jersey, Passenger and Crew Lists, 1956-1964* [database on-line]. Provo, UT, USA: Ancestry.com Operations, Inc., 2015.

Kingsley, Grace. "Flashes: Wally's Double – Arnold Gregg Signs with Harry Garson." *Los Angeles Times*, April 24, 1925.

Mitchell, Rory. *Historic-Cultural Monument Application for the home of Anna Zacsek, 2233 ½ W. Sunset Blvd, Cultural Heritage Commission, Los Angeles Department of City Planning. 2011.* Web. Accessed January 15, 2018. <http://cityplanning.lacity.org/StaffRpt/CHC/10-20-11/CHC-2011-2619.pdf>

Orlando Franklin Weber, Jr. *FindAGrave*. Web. Accessed December 17, 2018. < https://www.findagrave.com/memorial/86452945/orlando-franklin-weber>
Rodney L. Vaale, Ancestry.com. *California, Death Index, 1940-1997* [database on-line]. Provo, UT, USA: Ancestry.com Operations Inc, 2000.
Smith, Geraldine. "Frustration." *Philadelphia Inquirer*, June 7, 1942.
Stefan Zacsek, Year: *1940*; Census Place: *Los Angeles, Los Angeles, California*; Roll: *m-t0627-00378*; Page: *61A*; Enumeration District: *60-731*. Ancestry.com. *1940 United States Federal Census* [database on-line]. Provo, UT, USA: Ancestry.com Operations, Inc., 2012. Original data: United States of America, Bureau of the Census. *Sixteenth Census of the United States, 1940*. Washington, D.C.: National Archives and Records Administration, 1940. T627, 4,643 rolls.
Stephen Windsor [Istvan Kalman Kopcso], Ancestry.com. *U.S. Naturalization Record Indexes, 1791-1992 (Indexed in World Archives Project)* [database on-line]. Provo, UT, USA: Ancestry.com Operations, Inc., 2010.
Talbot, Steve. "Olga, Daughter of Unrest." *Photo-Play Journal*, June 1916.
Teresa Zacsek, Year: *1940*; Census Place: *Los Angeles, Los Angeles, California*; Roll: *m-t0627-00421*; Page: *1A*; Enumeration District: *60-1114*. Ancestry.com. *1940 United States Federal Census* [database on-line]. Provo, UT, USA: Ancestry.com Operations, Inc., 2012. Original data: United States of America, Bureau of the Census. *Sixteenth Census of the United States, 1940*. Washington, D.C.: National Archives and Records Administration, 1940. T627, 4,643 rolls.
Wilson, Margery (1956). *I Found My Way: An Autobiography*. J.B. Lippincott Company.

Rosa Rudami

"New York Passenger Arrival Lists (Ellis Island), 1892-1924", database with images, *FamilySearch* (https://familysearch.org/ark:/61903/1:1:JN3H-LTP : 30 January 2018), Maurice Rudomine, 1922.
"New York State Census, 1905," database with images, FamilySearch(https://familysearch.org/ark:/61903/1:1:SPXP-NQH : 20 July 2018), Petro Geovernali, Manhattan, A.D. 14, E.D. 10, New York, New York; citing p. 26, line 31, various county clerk offices, New York; FHL microfilm 1,433,089.
"New York, New York City Births, 1846-1909," database, *FamilySearch*(https://familysearch.org/ark:/61903/1:1:2WW4-9L3 : 11 February 2018), Reasalia Governali, 11 Dec 1898; citing Manhattan, New York, New York, United States, reference cn 48375 New York Municipal Archives, New York; FHL microfilm 1,953,370.
"New York, New York City Marriage Records, 1829-1940," database, *FamilySearch* (https://familysearch.org/ark:/61903/1:1:247X-GR2 : 10 February 2018), Maurice Rudomine and Rosalie Governali, 01 Nov 1919; citing Marriage, Manhattan, New York, New York, United States, New York City Municipal Archives, New York; FHL microfilm 1,643,530.

"United States World War I Draft Registration Cards, 1917-1918," database with images, *FamilySearch*(https://familysearch.org/ark:/61903/1:1:K6JC-GWH : 13 March 2018), Francisco Gonzalez Gamarra, 1917-1918; citing New York City no 158, New York, United States, NARA microfilm publication M1509 (Washington D.C.: National Archives and Records Administration, n.d.); FHL microfilm 1,786,820.

"A Poor Girl's Romance." Review. *Film Daily*, August 31, 1926.

"Actress to be Hostess to Newsies." *Los Angeles Times*, November 24, 1925.

"Biography." *Francisco Gonzalez Gamarra (1890-1972)*. Web. Accessed April 18, 2018. < http://fgonzalezgamarra.org/biograf_e.html>

"Bishop to Say Requiem Mass for Mrs. Fox." *Albany Times-Union* (NY), February 3, 1966.

"Bride Seeks Death After Anarchist Scorns Her Love." *New York Tribune*, November 10, 1919.

"Garfield Woman Makes Own Raid." *Passaic Daily Herald* (NJ), February 10, 1923.

"Girl Who Abandoned Baby Given Liberty." *Los Angeles Times*, May 3, 1928.

"Hollywood." *News-Chronicle* (Shippensburg, PA), June 15, 1928.

"Jimmy Fidler in Hollywood." *Santa Ana Register* (CA), July 8, 1936.

"Julia Governali Macaluso." *FindAGrave*. Web. Accessed November 6, 2018. < https://www.findagrave.com/memorial/19211977/julia-macaluso>

"Long Hair Still Popular in Film Colony in West." *Quad-City Times* (Davenport, IA), June 14, 1925.

"Made for Love." *AFI Catalog of Feature Films, The First 100 Years 1893-1993: American Film Institute*. Web. Accessed November 5, 2018. <http://catalog.afi.com/Catalog/MovieDetails/10506>

"Millionaire and Actress Bride." *St. Louis Post-Dispatch* (MO), October 6, 1928.

"Movieland by Jack Wooldridge." *Oakland Tribune* (CA), June 13, 1926.

"New Peruvian Artist." *Washington Herald* (DC), June 18, 1922.

"Only the Best Are Good Enough for Fox Films." *Fox Folks*, September 1926.

"Pete Governali Dies After Brief Illness." *Garfield Guardian* (NJ), February 8, 1963.

"Producer's Distribution Corp. Announces Releases For First Half of Coming Year's Program." *Moving Picture World*, December 26, 2915.

"Rosa Governali Fox." Obituary. *Albany Times-Union*, February 3, 1966.

"Rosa Rudami is Hostess." *Los Angeles Times*, February 7, 1926.

"Rosa Rudami Joines DeMille Studio Forces." *Motion Picture News*, June 20, 1925.

"Rosa Rudami Released." *Variety*, February 24, 1926.

"Rosa Rudimi [sic] Wants Estate of Father-in-Law Tallied." *Variety*, June 19, 1929.

"Screen News from Broadway." *Screenland*, January 1928.

"Seeks to Help East Patterson Kidnapper." *The Record* (Hackensack, NJ), March 6, 1925.

"Signed by Criterion Pictures." *Film Daily*, November 12, 1924.

"The Lily." *AFI Catalog of Feature Films, The First 100 Years 1893-1993: American Film Institute.* Web. Accessed November 5, 2018. <http://catalog.afi.com/Catalog/MovieDetails/10286>

"The Masked Dancer." Review. *Exhibitors Herald,* July 5, 1924.

"Three Faces East." *AFI Catalog of Feature Films, The First 100 Years 1893-1993: American Film Institute.* Web. Accessed November 5, 2018. <http://catalog.afi.com/Catalog/MovieDetails/12659>

"To Guide Aliens." *Press and Sun-Bulletin* (Binghampton, NY), February 19, 1942.

"Took Poison, Girl Says, When Urged to Anarchy." *Evening World* (New York, NY), November 10, 1919.

"Writes Song for F.B.O. Film." *Moving Picture World,* May 29, 1926.

Advertisement for Café Montmartre, *Los Angeles Times,* April 16, 1926.

Aleandri, Emelie (1999). *The Italian-American Immigrant Theatre of New York City (Images of America).* Arcadia Publishing Library Editions.

Arnold, Jeanne. "Just Wondering – Albanian Predicts PR's Choice." *Albany Times-Union* (NY), July 27, 1962.

Blurb about "Latin Lillian Gish," *Los Angeles Times,* May 2, 1926.

Francesca Damico, Ancestry.com. *New York, New York, Extracted Marriage Index, 1866-1937* [database on-line]. Provo, UT, USA: Ancestry.com Operations, Inc., 2014.

Gebhart, Myrtle. "Black Orchids, or What Have You?" *Picture-Play,* October 1926.

John V. Fox, Year: *1930*; Census Place: *Garfield, Bergen, New Jersey*; Page: *2A*; Enumeration District: *0091*; FHL microfilm: *2341048*. Ancestry.com. *1930 United States Federal Census* [database on-line]. Provo, UT, USA: Ancestry.com Operations Inc, 2002. Original data: United States of America, Bureau of the Census. *Fifteenth Census of the United States, 1930.* Washington, D.C.: National Archives and Records Administration, 1930. T626, 2,667 rolls.

Kingsley, Grace. "Halperins Sign Actress." *Los Angeles Times,* September 25, 1928.

McBride, Mary Margaret. "Sight Endangered, Star Quit Movies for New Career." *Longview News-Journal* (TX), May 31, 1936.

Moris Rudomene [sic], Year: *1920*; Census Place: *Manhattan Assembly District 17, New York, New York*; Roll: *T625_1217*; Page: *3B*; Enumeration District: *1216*. Ancestry.com. *1920 United States Federal Census* [database on-line]. Provo, UT, USA: Ancestry.com Operations, Inc., 2010. Images reproduced by FamilySearch. Original data: Fourteenth Census of the United States, 1920. (NARA microfilm publication T625, 2076 rolls). Records of the Bureau of the Census, Record Group 29. National Archives, Washington, D.C. Note: Enumeration Districts 819-839 are on roll 323 (Chicago City).

Nye, Myra. "Society of Cinemaland." *Los Angeles Times,* September 30, 1928.

Peter C. Fox, Year: *1940*; Census Place: *New York, New York, New York*; Roll: *m-t0627-02655*; Page: *18B*; Enumeration District: *31-1335*. Ancestry.com. *1940 United States Federal Census* [database on-line]. Provo, UT,

USA: Ancestry.com Operations, Inc., 2012. Original data: United States of America, Bureau of the Census. *Sixteenth Census of the United States, 1940.* Washington, D.C.: National Archives and Records Administration, 1940. T627, 4,643 rolls.

Philip Governali, Year: *1930*; Census Place: *Garfield, Bergen, New Jersey*; Page: *13B*; Enumeration District: *0091*; FHL microfilm: *2341048*. Ancestry.com. *1930 United States Federal Census* [database on-line]. Provo, UT, USA: Ancestry.com Operations Inc, 2002. Original data: United States of America, Bureau of the Census. *Fifteenth Census of the United States, 1930.* Washington, D.C.: National Archives and Records Administration, 1930. T626, 2,667 rolls.

Philip Governali, Year: *1940*; Census Place: *Garfield, Bergen, New Jersey*; Roll: *m-t0627-02308*; Page: *5B*; Enumeration District: *2-132*. Ancestry.com. *1940 United States Federal Census* [database on-line]. Provo, UT, USA: Ancestry.com Operations, Inc., 2012. Original data: United States of America, Bureau of the Census. *Sixteenth Census of the United States, 1940.* Washington, D.C.: National Archives and Records Administration, 1940. T627, 4,643 rolls.

Pierce, Max. "Russ Columbo: Hollywood's Tragic Crooner." *Classic Images*, April 1999.

Rosa Fox, Ancestry.com. *U.S., Social Security Death Index, 1935-2014* [database on-line]. Provo, UT, USA: Ancestry.com Operations Inc, 2014.

Rosalia Governale [sic], Year: *1900*; Census Place: *Manhattan, New York, New York*; Page: *2*; Enumeration District: *0335*; FHL microfilm: *1241096*. Ancestry.com. *1900 United States Federal Census* [database on-line]. Provo, UT, USA: Ancestry.com Operations Inc, 2004. Original data: United States of America, Bureau of the Census. *Twelfth Census of the United States, 1900.* Washington, D.C.: National Archives and Records Administration, 1900. T623, 1854 rolls.

Rose Governali, Year: *1910*; Census Place: *Manhattan Ward 17, New York, New York*; Roll: *T624_1033*; Page: *12B*; Enumeration District: *0924*; FHL microfilm: *1375046*. Ancestry.com. *1910 United States Federal Census* [database on-line]. Lehi, UT, USA: Ancestry.com Operations Inc, 2006. Original data: Thirteenth Census of the United States, 1910 (NARA microfilm publication T624, 1,178 rolls). Records of the Bureau of the Census, Record Group 29. National Archives, Washington, D.C

Stuyvesant, Isabel. "Society of Cinemaland." *Los Angeles Times*, February 28, 1926.

Untitled article about Rudami's first suicide attempt, *New York Tribune*, August 21, 1919.

Rosemary Theby

"An Offensive Picture." *Moving Picture News*, February 15, 1913.

"As Seen and Heard by Arthur Forde." Hollywood Filmograph, July 23, 1932.

"City Lights." *AFI Catalog of Feature Films, The First 100 Years 1893-1993: American Film Institute.* Web. Accessed May 10, 2018. <http://catalog.afi.com/Catalog/MovieDetails/3886>

"Harry Myers." *Another Nice Mess.* Web. Accessed May 10, 2018. <http://www.lordheath.com/menu1_658.html>

"Harry Myers." Obituary. *Variety*, December 28, 1938.

"Harry Myers' Funeral Today." *Los Angeles Times*, December 28, 1938.

"Henry C. Myers." *FindAGrave.* Web. Accessed May 10, 2018. < https://www.findagrave.com/memorial/34718181/henry-c_-myers>

"Houdini's Leading Ladies: Rosemary Theby." *Wild About Harry: Where Houdini Lives.* Web. Accessed May 10, 2018. <https://www.wildabouthoudini.com/2012/02/houdinis-leading-ladies-rosemary-theby.html>

"Kismet." *AFI Catalog of Feature Films, The First 100 Years 1893-1993: American Film Institute.* Web. Accessed May 10, 2018. <http://catalog.afi.com/Catalog/MovieDetails/17865>

"Miss Rosemary Theby." *Moving Picture World*, April 13, 1912.

"One Million B.C." *AFI Catalog of Feature Films, The First 100 Years 1893-1993: American Film Institute.* Web. Accessed May 10, 2018. <http://catalog.afi.com/Catalog/MovieDetails/5130>

"Rosemary Theby." *Motion Picture*, October 1914.

"Rosemary Theby." *Silent Hollywood.* Web. Accessed May 10, 2018. <https://silenthollywood.com/rosemarytheby.html>

"Rosemary Theresa Theby." *FindAGrave.* Web. Accessed May 10, 2018. <https://www.findagrave.com/memorial/140947837/rosemary-theresa-theby>

"Tea With a Kick." Review. *Pictures and the Picturegoer*, August 1924.

"Terror Island." Review. *Film Daily*, May 2, 1920.

"The Fatal Glass of Beer." *AFI Catalog of Feature Films, The First 100 Years 1893-1993: American Film Institute.* Web. Accessed May 10, 2018. <http://catalog.afi.com/Catalog/MovieDetails/67299>

"The Fatal Glass of Beer." Review. *Film Daily*, June 3, 1933.

"The Red Lily." Review. *Film Daily*, August 3. 1924.

"Trial Marriage." *AFI Catalog of Feature Films, The First 100 Years 1893-1993: American Film Institute.* Web. Accessed May 10, 2018. <http://catalog.afi.com/Catalog/MovieDetails/12832>

"When 'Rose' Became Little 'Rose Mary'." *Des Moines Tribune* (IA), November 10, 1921.

Carr, Caroline. "How Necessity Made This Star Successful." *Oakland Tribune* (CA), May 30, 1915.

Certificate of Death: Arthur J. Theby. Filed November 22, 1912, State of Missouri, County (absent), Dept. of Health, Reg. Dist. No. 791-37793, State File No. (absent). Informant: Louis Theby [parent].

Certificate of Death: Louis G. Theby. Filed October 18,1953, State of Missouri, County (absent), Dept. of Health, Reg. Dist. No. 318-37652, State File No. (absent). Informant: Mamie R. Theby [spouse].

Certificate of Death: Rosemary Hughes. Filed November 10, 1973, State of California, County of Los Angeles, Dept. of Health, Reg. Dist. No. 7097-046333, State File No. (absent). Informant: Truitt Hughes [spouse].

Daly, Phil M. "Along the Rialto." *Film Daily,* June 24, 1938.

Gifford, Denis (1969). *Movie Monsters.* Littlehampton Book Services Ltd., 1st Edition.

Harrison, Paul. "Film Industry Casting Several in Minor Roles." *Rochester Times-Union* (New York), March 26, 1936.

Harry C. Myers, Ancestry.com. *California, Death Index, 1905-1939* [database on-line]. Provo, UT, USA: Ancestry.com Operations, Inc., 2013.

Harry Myers, Year: *1930*; Census Place: *Egg Harbor Township, Atlantic, New Jersey*; Page: *6A*; Enumeration District: *0043*; FHL microfilm: *2341044*. Ancestry.com. *1930 United States Federal Census* [database on-line]. Provo, UT, USA: Ancestry.com Operations Inc, 2002. Original data: United States of America, Bureau of the Census. *Fifteenth Census of the United States, 1930*. Washington, D.C.: National Archives and Records Administration, 1930. T626, 2,667 rolls.

Henry Clifford Myers, Registration State: *Pennsylvania*; Registration County: *Philadelphia*; Roll: *1907767*; Draft Board: *43*. Ancestry.com. *U.S., World War I Draft Registration Cards, 1917-1918* [database on-line]. Provo, UT, USA: Ancestry.com Operations Inc, 2005. Original data: United States, Selective Service System. *World War I Selective Service System Draft Registration Cards, 1917-1918*. Washington, D.C.: National Archives and Records Administration. M1509, 4,582 rolls.

Keavy, Hubbard. "Screen Life in Hollywood." *Plattsburg Daily Press* (NY), January 12, 1932.

Lahue, Kalton C. (1966). *World of Laughter: The Motion Picture Comedy Short, 1910-1930.* University of Oklahoma Press.

Lipke, Katherine. "What a Nice Vampire!" *Los Angeles Times*, September 21, 1924.

Lorenzo Myers, National Archives and Records Administration (NARA); Washington D.C.; Volume #: *Volume 12: Special Series - New York.* Ancestry.com. *U.S. Passport Applications, 1795-1925* [database on-line]. Lehi, UT, USA: Ancestry.com Operations, Inc., 2007. Original data: *Selected Passports*. National Archives, Washington, D.C.

Louis Thely [sic], Year: *1910*; Census Place: *St Louis Ward 27, Saint Louis City, Missouri*; Roll: *T624_819*; Page: *5B*; Enumeration District: *0424*; FHL microfilm: *1374832*. Ancestry.com. *1910 United States Federal Census* [database on-line]. Lehi, UT, USA: Ancestry.com Operations Inc, 2006. Original data: Thirteenth Census of the United States, 1910 (NARA microfilm publication T624, 1,178 rolls). Records of the Bureau of the Census, Record Group 29. National Archives, Washington, D.C.

Rose Mary [sic] Myers, Year: *1930*; Census Place: *Los Angeles, Los Angeles, California*; Page: *11A*; Enumeration District: *0179*; FHL microfilm: *2339875*. Ancestry.com. *1930 United States Federal Census* [database on-line]. Provo,

UT, USA: Ancestry.com Operations Inc, 2002. Original data: United States of America, Bureau of the Census. *Fifteenth Census of the United States, 1930*. Washington, D.C.: National Archives and Records Administration, 1930. T626, 2,667 rolls.

Rosemary Hughes, Ancestry.com. *California, Death Index, 1940-1997* [database on-line]. Provo, UT, USA: Ancestry.com Operations Inc, 2000.

Rosemary Hughes, Ancestry.com. *U.S., Social Security Death Index, 1935-2014* [database on-line]. Provo, UT, USA: Ancestry.com Operations Inc, 2014.

Rosemary Teby [sic], Missouri State Archives; Jefferson City, MO, USA; *Missouri Birth Records [Microfilm]*. Ancestry.com. *Missouri, Birth Registers, 1847-1910* [database on-line]. Provo, UT, USA: Ancestry.com Operations, Inc., 2007. Original data: *Missouri Birth Records [Microfilm]*. Jefferson City, MO, USA: Missouri State Archives.

Rosemary Theby, Year: *1920*; Census Place: *Los Angeles Assembly District 63, Los Angeles, California*; Roll: *T625_106*; Page: *5A*; Enumeration District: *163*. Ancestry.com. *1920 United States Federal Census* [database on-line]. Provo, UT, USA: Ancestry.com Operations, Inc., 2010. Images reproduced by FamilySearch. Original data: Fourteenth Census of the United States, 1920. (NARA microfilm publication T625, 2076 rolls). Records of the Bureau of the Census, Record Group 29. National Archives, Washington, D.C. Note: Enumeration Districts 819-839 are on roll 323 (Chicago City).

Schallert, Edwin. "Rosemary and Reminiscences." *Los Angeles Times*, May 2, 1920.

Schallert, Elza. "What Makes a Perfect Marriage?" *Picture-Play*, February 1927.

Sullivan, Ed. "HOLLYWOOD: An Extra's Letter to Her Ma." *Harrisburg Telegraph* (PA), November 11, 1937.

Thompson, Frank (1996). *Lost Films: Important Movies That Disappeared*. Citadel Press.

Truitt W. Hughes, Ancestry.com. *U.S. City Directories, 1822-1995* [database on-line]. Provo, UT, USA: Ancestry.com Operations, Inc., 2011.

Truitt W. Hughes, Year: *1930*; Census Place: *Los Angeles, Los Angeles, California*; Page: *75A*; Enumeration District: *0616*; FHL microfilm: *2339893*. Ancestry.com. *1930 United States Federal Census* [database on-line]. Provo, UT, USA: Ancestry.com Operations Inc, 2002. Original data: United States of America, Bureau of the Census. *Fifteenth Census of the United States, 1930*. Washington, D.C.: National Archives and Records Administration, 1930. T626, 2,667 rolls.

Whitaker, Alma. "Vampire is Normal Off Screen." *Los Angeles Times*, July 13, 1924.

York, Cal. "Studio News & Gossip East & West." *Photoplay*, April 1926.

Ruth Taylor

"Anita Picks Ruth, Blonde." *Hollywood Vagabond*, September 8, 1927.
"Austin With New Team." *Los Angeles Times*, May 26, 1928.

"Dangerous Curves Behind." Review. *Film Daily*, November 15, 1925.
"Ex-actress dead." *Desert Sun* (Palm Springs, CA), April 16, 1984.
"Four Residences on Home Tour Itinerary." *Los Angeles Times*, February 26, 1968.
"Gentlemen Prefer Blondes." *AFI Catalog of Feature Films, The First 100 Years 1893-1993: American Film Institute.* Web. Accessed September 15, 2018. <http://catalog.afi.com/Catalog/MovieDetails/9315>
"Gentlemen Prefer Blondes." *Exhibitors Herald and Moving Picture World*, March 17, 1928.
"Has No Competition." *Los Angeles Times*, March 6, 1925.
"INTRODUCING: Ruth Taylor." *Hollywood Vagabond*, November 3, 1927.
"Paramount." *Moving Picture World Hollywood Office*, September 24, 1927.
"Paul S. Zuckerman, Broker Here, Was 66." *New York Times*, December 4, 1965.
"Pick 'Lorelei'." *Moving Picture World,* August 27, 1927.
"Questions & Answers." *Photoplay*, April 1931.
"Ruth Lee Taylor [sic], Cast for 'Lorelei', A Sennett Girl." *Moving Picture World*, September 10, 1927.
"Ruth Taylor Has Leading Role in Mack Sennett Comedy." *Exhibitors Trade Review*, April 18, 1925.
"Ruth Taylor In It." *Los Angeles Times*, December 20, 1928.
"Ruth Taylor Steps Up." *Moving Picture World,* June 26, 1926.
"Ruth Taylor." *FindAGrave*. Web. Accessed January 31, 2018. <https://www.findagrave.com/memorial/11698510/ruth-taylor>
"Ruth Taylor." *Hollywood Vagabond*, December 1, 1927.
"Ruth Taylor." *Silent Era*. Web. Accessed November 20, 2018. <http://www.silentera.com/people/actresses/Taylor-Ruth.html>
"Screen Lorelei Suffers Illness." *Los Angeles Times*, September 3, 1928.
"She's in Pictures, All Right." *Los Angeles Times*, November 1, 1927.
"Tattletale." *Los Angeles Times*, August 3, 1941.
"What the Fans Think." *Picture-Play*, August 1928.
"What the Fans Think." *Picture-Play*, July 1928.
"Zuckerman." Obituary. *Desert Sun* (Palm Springs, CA), April 17, 1984.
Arthur, Allene. "Big doings for wee critters." *Desert Sun* (Palm Springs, CA), October 14, 1983.
Bell, Caroline. "Thorns in a Bed of Roses." *Picture Play*, March 1931.
Berry, Leonard J. "Buck Henry Rises to Surface, Finds That It's Glaring." *Los Angeles Times*, April 25, 1971.
Bland. "Along The Line: Making 'Em White." *Variety*, January 18, 1928.
Bystander, The. "Over the Teacups." *Picture-Play*, December 1927.
Bystander, The. "Over the Teacups." *Picture-Play*, March 1928.
Cox, Rosemary. "Zuckerman Desert Hideaway Brings the Outdoors Inside." *Desert Sun* (Palm Springs, CA), March 5 1976.
Daly, Phil M. "Along the Rialto." *Film Daily*, October 19, 1931.
Duke, Mabel. "Come Out of the Kitchen." *Picture Play*, March 1931.

Gray, Beverly (2017). *Seduced by Mrs. Robinson: How "The Graduate" Became the Touchstone of a Generation*. Algonquin Books.
Hall, Mordaunt. "The Screen; Lorelei Lee and Dorothy." *New York Times*, January 16, 1928.
Ivah Taylor, Ancestry.com. *U.S. City Directories, 1822-1995* [database on-line]. Provo, UT, USA: Ancestry.com Operations, Inc., 2011.
Larkin, Mark. "Don't Be Discovered." *Photoplay*, April 1929.
Lusk, Nobert. "The Screen in Review." *Picture-Play*, April 1928.
McIntyre, O.O. "New York Day by Day." *San Francisco Examiner*, October 15, 1930.
Mook, Richard. "They Got What They Wanted, But –." *Picture Play*, December 1929.
Norman C. Taylor, Year: *1930*; Census Place: *Beverly Hills, Los Angeles, California*; Page: *4B*; Enumeration District: *0840*; FHL microfilm: *2339859*. Ancestry.com. *1930 United States Federal Census* [database on-line]. Provo, UT, USA: Ancestry.com Operations Inc, 2002. Original data: United States of America, Bureau of the Census. *Fifteenth Census of the United States, 1930*. Washington, D.C.: National Archives and Records Administration, 1930. T626, 2,667 rolls.
Norman Taylor, Year: *1940*; Census Place: *Los Angeles, Los Angeles, California*; Roll: *m-t0627-00404*; Page: *14A*; Enumeration District: *60-173*. Ancestry.com. *1940 United States Federal Census* [database on-line]. Provo, UT, USA: Ancestry.com Operations, Inc., 2012. Original data: United States of America, Bureau of the Census. *Sixteenth Census of the United States, 1940*. Washington, D.C.: National Archives and Records Administration, 1940. T627, 4,643 rolls.
O'Brian, Jack. "British Whodunit Draws Smart Set." *Journal News* (White Plains, NY), November 17, 1970.
Parsons, Louella. Syndicated column, *Anderson Daily Bulletin* (Anderson, IN), October 11, 1965.
Robb, Inez. "Blondes Still Preferred." *Cincinnati Enquirer*, July 30, 1939.
Romero, Ramón. "Parade of the Cinderellas." *New Movie Magazine*, October 1933.
Ruth A. Taylor, Year: *1910*; Census Place: *Portland Ward 5, Multnomah, Oregon*; Roll: *T624_1286*; Page: *4B*; Enumeration District: *0168*; FHL microfilm: *1375299*. Ancestry.com. *1910 United States Federal Census* [database on-line]. Lehi, UT, USA: Ancestry.com Operations Inc, 2006. Original data: Thirteenth Census of the United States, 1910 (NARA microfilm publication T624, 1,178 rolls). Records of the Bureau of the Census, Record Group 29. National Archives, Washington, D.C.
Ruth Alice Taylor, Year: *1920*; Census Place: *Portland, Multnomah, Oregon*; Roll: *T625_1502*; Page: *13B*; Enumeration District: *138*. Ancestry.com. *1920 United States Federal Census* [database on-line]. Provo, UT, USA: Ancestry.com Operations, Inc., 2010. Images reproduced by FamilySearch. Original data: Fourteenth Census of the United States, 1920. (NARA microfilm

publication T625, 2076 rolls). Records of the Bureau of the Census, Record Group 29. National Archives, Washington, D.C. Note: Enumeration Districts 819-839 are on roll 323 (Chicago City).

Ruth T. Zuckerman, Ancestry.com. *New York, New York, Marriage License Indexes, 1907-2018* [database on-line]. Lehi, UT, USA: Ancestry.com Operations, Inc., 2017.

Ruth Taylor Zuckerman, Ancestry.com. *California, Death Index, 1940-1997* [database on-line]. Provo, UT, USA: Ancestry.com Operations Inc, 2000.

Story, Jackie. "'Museum Follower' Seeking Members." *Desert Sun* (Palm Springs, CA), April 18, 1984.

Thomas, Phil. "'Get Smart' Author Talks of Writing, Acting, Life." *Marshall News Messenger* (TX), May 13, 1971.

Thompson, Frank (1996). *Lost Films: Important Movies That Disappeared*. Citadel Press.

Walker, Brent E. (2009). *Mack Sennett's Fun Factory: A History and Filmography of His Studio and His Keystone and Mack Sennett Comedies, with Biographies of Players and Personnel, Vols. 1 & 2*. McFarland.

Waterbury, Ruth. "The Search for Lorelei Lee." *Photoplay*, November 1927.

Index

"Zoot Suit Riots" *see* Sleepy Lagoon Murder Trial
A Connecticut Yankee at King Arthur's Court (1920) 91
A Deaf Burglar (1913) 10
A Diplomat Interrupted (1912) 50
A Fool There Was (1916) 10
A Hint to Brides (1929) 103
A Poor Girl's Romance (1926) 82
A Question of Right (1914) 90
A Six Shootin' Romance (1926) 13
A Star is Born (1937) 34
Absentee, The (1915) 70
Adventures of Marguerite, The (1915-1916 film series) 1
Aitken, Spottiswoode 23, 70
Alden, Mary 3, 70
All Quiet on the Western Front (1930) 62
All SOuls' Eve (1920) 12
All's Fair in Love (1921) 62
American Releasing Corp. 33, 62
Ankewich, Camille *see* Marcia Manon
Arbuckle, Roscoe "Fatty" 13
Arizona Kid, The (1930) 35
Arthur, Johnny 103-104
As You Like It (1912) 89
Associated Producers 62-63, 92
Astor, Mary 22
August, Edwin 33, 50-51,
Average Woman, The (1924) 34, 81
Baggot, King 14
Bara, Theda *vii*, 10, 20, 32, 59
Barriscale, Bessie 61, 63, 73
Barrymore, John 22, 61, **66**, 72
Barrymore, Lionel 21, 43-44, 72
Baxter, Warner 35
Beau Brummel (1924) 22
Beery, Noah 12
Beery, Wallace 41, 93
Belasco 82, 84, 92
Bellamy, Madge 4
Bennett, Constance 22, 104
Berger, Rosalie *see* Alice Hollister
Bernstein, Dr. Montrose 25-26
Big Parade, The (1925) 62
Biograph 1
Bird of Paradise (1932) 73
Birth of a Nation, The (1915) 69, 71
Block Heads (1938) 94
Blonde Vampire, The (1920 book) 32
Blonde Vampire, The (1922) 33, **39**
Blood and Sand (1922) 22
Blythe, Betty 20, 35
Bosworth, Hobart 49
Bow, Clara 21, 42, 102-103
Breamer, Sylvia 84, 92
Bright Lights of Broadway (1923) 21
Bright's Disease 1, 4
Broadway Nights (1927) 34
Brockwell, Gladys 70, 93
Brooks, Louise 24, 102
Browning, Tod 41, 43-44, 71
Busch, Mae 4
By a Woman's Wit (1911) 2
By Whose Hand? (1927) 34
Cabaret Girl, The (1918) 10
Calvary Cemetery [California] 74
Captain Fearless (1925) 22
Captain Kidd Jr. (1919) 61
Cassidy of the Air Lanes see *Great Air Robbery, The*
Cassinelli, Dolores 32-33
Chadwick, Helene 22, 81,
Challenge, The (1922) 3
Chaney, Lon 10, 44
Chaplin, Charles 94
Charge of the Light Brigade, The (1926) 45

Chase, Charley 10
Chased into Love (1917) 10
Children of the Ghetto (1910 play) 69
City Lights (1931) 94
Cloud-Puncher, The (1917) 10
Coast Patrol, The (1925) 23
Cobra (1925) 23
Cody, Lew 22
Colleen Bawn, The (1911) 2
College Coquette, The (1929) 103
Collier, Carmen *see* Carmen Phillips
Collier, Constance 70
Colman, Ronald 22
Colombo, Russell *see* Russ Columbo
Columbia 34, 45, 103, 105
Columbo, Russ 82
Conklin, Chester 92, 102
Coquette, The (1911) 49
Costello, Dolores 22
Courtot, Marguerite 1, 3
Dancers, The (1925) 4
Dangerous Curves Behind (1925) 102
Dante's Inferno (1924) 63
Dark Rosaleen (1919 play) 31
Darmond, Grace 14
Day, Alice 101, 103
de la Motte, Marguerite 11, 63, 69
De Lorez, Claire **18**, 19-26, **27-29**
Dean, Priscilla 34, 41
Death Valley Days (1952–1970) 53
DeMille, Cecil B. 61, 81, 83-84
Denny, Reginald 22
Dentist, The (1932) 73
Desert Memorial Park [California] 105
Desmond, William 11
Deutch, Claire *see* Claire de Lorez
Devil-Stone, The (1917) 62
Double Trouble (1915) 70
Drifter, The (1916) 51-52
Drifting (1923) 41
Drown, Hope 13, 104
Duzan, Frances *see* Edna Tichenor
Eddy, Helen Jerome 62-63, 69
Educational Screen (magazine) 20, 22

Egan Institute of Dramatic Art *see* Egan Theater
Egan Theater 69, 72-73
Eis and French 3, **138**
El Kalem (unit) *see* Kalem
Enemies of Women (1923) 21
Essanay 36
Exhibitors Mutual 11
Fair Week (1924) 13
Fair, Elinor 81, 91, 95
Fairbanks Sr., Douglas 70
Famous Players-Lasky 1, 10-13, 60-61, 63, 102
Farnum, William 20, 93
Fatal Glass of Beer, The (1933) 94
Father's Close Shave (1920) 20
FBO 22, 32, 81-82
Fields, W.C. 73, 94
Fight Against Evil, The (1913) 50
Film Daily (magazine) 12, 21, 43, 72, 81, 91-93, 103-104
Film Fun (magazine) 4
First National 22, 33-34, 62, 91-92
Fisher, Margarita 50, 71,
For a Woman's Honor (1919) 11
Forbidden Paths (1917) 10
Forbidden Thing, The (1920) 62
Forbidden Waters (1926) 34
Ford, Harrison 21, 34, 42
Forest Lawn Memorial Park [California] 5
Forgotten Law, The (1923) 4
Four Horsemen of the Apocalypse, The (1921) 20-21
Fox 2, 4, 10, 20-21, 35-36, 43, 62, 63, 81-82, 91, 101
Fox, John Conway 84
Fox, Rosa *see* Rosa Rudami
Franco Films 23-24
Frederick, Pauline 4
From the Manger to the Cross; or, *Jesus of Nazareth* (1913) 2, 5, 71
Front Page, The (1931) 74
Frothingham, J.L. 62-63

Gamarra, Rosina González *see* Rosa Rudami
Gaumont 52
Gauntier, Gene 2-3
Gentlemen Prefer Blondes (1928) 102, **106**
Gentlemen Prefer Blondes: The Intimate Diary of a Professional Lady (1925 book) 102
Get Smart (1965-1970) 105
Gilbert, John 4, 11, 43, 62
Girl at Home, The (1917) 71
Girl of the Golden West, The (1923) 92
Girl Shy (1924) 42
Girton, Perry 49, 53
Glaum, Louise *vii*
Glyn, Elinor 4, 21, 26
Gold Diggers of 1933 (1933) 42
Gold Diggers of Broadway (1929) 42
Gold Diggers, The (1923) 42
Goldwyn *see* M-G-M
Gosh-Darn Mortgage, The (1926) 43
Goudal, Jetta 81
Governali, Rosalia *see* Rosa Rudami
Graduate, The (1967) 105
Graves, Ralph 11, 101, 103
Gray, Arnold *see* Arnold Gregg
Great Air Robbery, The (1919) 12
Great Circus Mystery, The (1925 serial) 13
Great K & A Train Robbery, The (1926) 36
Great Love, The (1918) 90
Greater Glory, The (1926) 62
Gregg, Arnold -3
Grey, Olga *see* Anna Zacsek
Griffith, Corrine 10
Griffith, D.W. 71, 90, 94
Hale, Creighton 82, 92, 94
Hall, Mordaunt 24, 102
Hand That Rules the World, The (1914) 51
Hardy, Oliver 94
Harrison, Elizabeth *see* Marcia Manon

Harrison, Julian 59, 63-64
Haunted Manor, The (1916) 52-53, **57**
Hawk's Trail, The (1919-1920 serial) 14
Hawley, Wanda 12-13
Hayakawa, Sessue 10
Hazards of Helen, The (1914-1917 film series) 2
Heart Specialist, The (1922) 12
Heaven Can Wait (1978) 105
Heaven on Earth (1927) 62
Hell's Angels (1930) 74
Heller in Pink Tights (1960) 45
Henry, Buck 105
Her Night of Romance (1924) 22
Hersholt, Jean 22, 93
Hickory Farm (1906 play) 49
His Lesson (1915) 69
His Own Blood (1913) 50
Hollister Jr., George 2, 5
Hollister Sr., George 1-3, 5
Hollister, Alice *viii*, 1-5, **6-7**, 71, 109-112
Hollister, Doris Ethel 2, 5
Hollywood (1923) 13
Hollywood Filmograph (magazine) 24
Hollywood Forever Cemetery [California] 73
Holmes, Helen 2
Holt, Jack 12, 45, 61
Home Town Girl, The (1919) 11
Hope Diamond Mystery, The (1921 serial) 14
Hostage, The (1917) 60
Hotel Imperial (1928 play) 73-74
Houdini 91
Hoxie, Jack 13
Hughes, Howard 74
Hughes, Truitt 95
I Love Lucy (1951-1957) 53-54
In Old Arizona (1929) 35
In Slavery Days (1913) 50

Inglewood Park Cemetery [California] 54, 64
Intolerance (1916) 70
Iron Nag, The (1925) 101
It Is the Law (1924) 81
Jessel, George 62
Jim Bludso (1917) 71
Johnston, Julianne 22
Joy, Leatrice 53, 62, 81
Joyce, Alice 2
Joyous Trouble-Makers, The (1920) 20
Jungle Trail of the Son of Tarzan (1923) 33
Just Married (1928) 103
Just Off Broadway (1929) 35
Justice of the Far North (1925) 62
Kalem 1-3, 5
Karloff, Boris 14, 73
Kathan, Daniel 59
Kenyon, Doris 21, 52
Kerrigan, J. Warren 10, 13, 63, 92
Keystone 10, 61
King Kong (1933) 73
King of Kings, The (1927) 63
Kismet (1920) 91
Kleine, George 1
Kongo (1932) 44
Kopcso, Istvan 74
La Marr, Barbara 41, 63
La Plante, Laura 20, 104
La venenosa (1928) 24
Ladies Must Live (1921) 62
Langdon, Harry 94, 101
Lantz, Walter 5
Lasky *see* Famous Players-Lasky
Le soleil de minuit (1926) 23
Leonard, Robert Z. 50
L'Equipage (1928) 24
Lewis, Harry L. 35-36
Life's Twist (1920) 62
Lily, The (1926) 82
Little Theater *see* Egan Theater
Live Oak Memorial Park [California] 15
Lombard, Carole 35, 82

London After Midnight (1927) 43, 92
Long, Samuel 1
Loos, Anita 102, 104
Lord John's Journal (1915 serial) 13
Los Angeles Times 9, 14, 83, 94
Lotus Woman, The (1916) 3, **7**
Love, Live and Laugh (1929) 62
Lubin 90, 94
Lucky Stars (1925) 101
Macbeth (1916) 70
Made for Love (1926) 81
Majestic 69
Make Way for Tomorrow (1937) 94
Mann, Hank 10, 92
Manon, Marcia **58**, 59-64, **65-67**
Marion, Frank J. 1
Mark of the Vampire (1935) 44
Married Flirts (1924) 4
Martin, Vivian 10-11, 71
Masked Dancer, The (1924) 81
Maytime (1923) 42
McGowan, J.P. 2
McKee, Raymond 42, 101
Merry Widow, The (1925) 43
Metro *see* M-G-M
M-G-M (Metro-Goldwyn-Mayer) 4, 22, 42-43, 62, 92
Midnight Daddies (1930) 93
Milestones (1920) 3, **7**
Millarde, Harry 2-3
Miller, Raquel 24-25
Minter, Mary Miles 12
Mix, Tom 20, 36
Mong, William 41, 62, 92
Mooers, De Sacia **30**, 31-36, **37-39**, 81
Mooers, Douglas 31
Mooers, Edwin Demarest 31, 35
Moore, Colleen 92-93
Moore, Tom 2, 42
Morgane la sirene (1928) 23-24, **29**
Morosco Theater 53, 72
Most Dangerous Game, The (1932) 73
Motion Picture (magazine) 10, 41, 53, 59, 61, 63

Motion Picture Classic (magazine) 63
Motion Picture News (magazine) 11, 33, 43, 102, 104
Movie Weekly (magazine) 35
Moving Picture World (magazine) 3, 50-51, 61, 70, 72
Mrs. Temple's Telegram (1920) 12
Mulhall, Jack 4
Murray, Mae 4, 43,
Mutual 10, 51, 52, 69-70
My Wife and I (1925) 22
Myers, Carmel 22, 69
Myers, Harry 90-95, **97**
Myers-Theby Comedies 90, 93, **97**
Mystery Mind, The (1920) 32
Mystery of 13, The (1919 serial) 90
Nagel, Conrad 21, 44, 94
Naldi, Nita *vii*, 23
Nan the Confederate Spy (1909-1910) 2
Napoleon (1927) 23
Nazimova, Alla 62, 73
Negri, Pola *vii*
Nestor 10, 90
Net, The (1923) 21
New Adventures of Terence O' Rourke, The (1915 film series) 13
New York Times 24, 102
Northern Code, The (1925) 22
Novarro, Ramón 41, 92
Oberlander, Heinrich *see* Henry West
O'Brien, George 4
Oddfellows Cemetery [California] 75
Officer of the Day (1926) 43
O'Kalem (unit) *see* Kalem
Olcott, Sidney 1-3, 5
Old Wives for New (1918) 61
One Million B.C. (1940) 94
One More American (1918) 61
One Night in Rome (1924) 42
Pagan God, The (1919) 11
Paramount 1, 10-13, 23, 45, 51, 61-62, 71, 90-91, 102-104

Parrott, Charles *see* Charley Chase
Pathé 20, 43, 63, 71-72, 90, 101, 104
Phillips, Anna Catherine *see* Carmen Phillips
Phillips, Carmen **8**, 9-15, **16-17**
Photoplay (magazine) 5, 24, 35, 104
Pickford, Jack 71
Pickford, Mary 60-61
Picture-Play (magazine) 83, 103
Piff, Paff, Pouf (1909 play) 9
Pipes of Pan, The (1914) 10
Pitts, Zasu 22, 92
Potash and Perlmutter (1923) 33
Powers Picture Plays 50
Principal Pictures 21-22, 81
Pringle, Aileen 4, 21,
Prison Without Walls, The (1917) 59
Producers Distributing Corp. 22, 34, 81
Prouders 22, 61
Queen of Sheba, The (1921) 20
Range Terror, The (1925) 22
Realart 12
Re-Creation of Brian Kent, The (1925) 22
Red Lily, The (1924) 92
Reid, Wallace 13, 60
Reincarnation of Karma, The (1912) 89-90
Reliance 90
Rex 10, 50
Ridgley, Cleo 4
Robertson-Cole 91
Robot Monster (1953) 45
Rock, Allen 32, 35
Rubens, Alma 4, 21,
Rudami, Rosa **78**, 79-85, **86-87**
Rudomine, Maurice 79-80
Sacrifice, The (1911) 89
Samberg, Arnold *see* Arnold Gregg
San Francisco (1936) 94
San Francisco Call 19
Santschi, Tom 49, 93
Saturday Night Live (1975-) 105

Saville, Franc'Anna *see* De Sacia Mooers
Saville, Franc'Annie *see* De Sacia Mooers
Saville, Ruby 31, 34, 36
Saville, Ruth 31, 33, 36
Scarface (1932) 74
Schindler, Rudolph 74
Scrappily Married (1930) 104
Scuttlers, The (1920) 20
Selig 49-50
Sennett, Mack 43, 63, 93, 101-102
Shafer, Iva *see* Iva Shepard
Shafer, Pearl 49, 53-54
She (1935) 73
Shearer, Norma 4
Shepard, Iva **48**, 49-54, **55-57**
Sherman, Lowell 21, 81
Show, The (1927) 43
Silent Accuser, The (1924) 42
Silent Mystery, The (1918-1919 serial) 90
Sills, Milton 4, 61
Siren of Seville, The (1924) 22
Skin Deep (1922) 62
Skywayman, The (1920) 12
Sleepy Lagoon Murder Trial 73
Smouldering Fires (1915) 10
So Big (1924) 92
So This is Marriage (1924) 22
Son of Tarzan (1920-1921 serial) 32
Springer, Robert Joaquin 41
St. Agnes Cemetery [New York] 85
Stanwyck, Barbara 34
State Rights 14, 34, 93
Stella Maris (1918) 60, **65**
Sterling, Ford 94, 102,
Stone, Lewis 3
Straight Road, The (1914) 51
Street of Seven Stars, The (1918) 52
Sultan of Sulu, The (1909 play) 9
Susan Lenox: Her Fall and Rise (1931) 45
Sydney, Sylvia 34
Talmadge, Constance 22, 71
Tangled Web, The (1913) 90
Taylor, Ruth **100**, 101-105, **106-107**
Tea—With a Kick! (1923) 92
Ten Nights in a Barroom (1931) 93-94
Terror Island (1920) 91
Test of Honor, The (1919) 61, **66**
Thanhouser 5
That Was the Week That Was (1964-1965) 105
Theby, Rosemary 22, **88**, 89-95, **96-99**
There's Many a Fool (1917) 10
Third Eye, The (1920 serial) 72
Thirty Days (1923) 13
This Thing Called Love (1929) 104
Three Faces East (1926) 81
Three Weeks (1924) 21
Tichenor, Edna **40**, 41-45, **46-47**
Tiger Woman, The (1917) 10
Tourneur, Maurice 24
Tree, Sir Herbert Beerbohm 70
Triangle 70-72
Trixie from Broadway (1919) 71, **77**
Twentieth Century (1934) 73
Uncle Tom's Cabin (1913) 5
Under the Rouge (1925) 22, 25
United Artists 63, 94
Universal 10, 12-13, 22, 41, 50-51, 90, 101
Upstairs and Down (1919) 91
Valentino, Rudolph 20, 23
Vampire, The (1913) 3
Variety (magazine) 24, 34, 51, 61, 70-71, 91, 102-103
Victor 10, 90
Victory of Conscience, The (1916) 59
Vidor, Florence 10, 61
Vignola, Robert 1-2
Virtuous Model, The (1919) 32
Vitagraph 1-3, 10, 32, 89,
Vogues of 1938 (1937) 94
Volga Boatman, The (1926) 81
Walthall, Henry B. 44, 81
Warner Bros. 22, 42, 45, 101

Warner, H.B. 11
Weber Jr., Orlando 74
Wedding Song, The (1925) 81, **87**
West of Zanzibar (1928) 44
West, Henry 45
Westwood Memorial Park [California] 95
Where East Is East (1929) 44
Whitewashed Walls (1919) 11
Wife of Marcius, The (1910) 49
Wild Party, The (1929) 103
Wilson, Lois 13, 34
Wilson, Margery 70, 72
Windsor, Stephen *see* Istvan Kopcso
Woman He Loved, The (1922) 62
Woman Michael Married, The (1919) 61
Wong, Anna May 41
Wray, Fay 23, 45
Yellow Girl, The (1916) 10, **16**
You Can't Take It with You (1938) 94
Zacsek, Anna **68**, 69-75, **76-77**
Zacsek, Teresa 69, 72, 74
Zenobia (1939) 94
Zuckerman, Henry *see* Buck Henry
Zuckerman, Paul 104
Zuckerman, Ruth *see* Ruth Taylor

About the Author

Jennifer Ann Redmond found her calling at age seven, when her essay won a countywide contest. Since then, her passion for writing has been rivaled only by her love of the 1920s and 1930s. Silent and pre-Code (1929-1934) films are a particular favorite, and she counts Clara Bow, Louise Brooks, and Jean Harlow among her muses. Her work has been featured in *Classic Images*, *Atlas Obscura*, and several other publications, as well as the Library of Congress website. Her first book, *Reels & Rivals: Sisters in Silent Film*, was voted one of the best film books of 2016 by Thomas Gladysz (Louise Brooks Society and *Huffington Post*). Her second, *Southern Belle to Hollywood Hell: Corliss Palmer and Her Scandalous Rise and Fall*, was *Classic Images'* 2018 winner for "Best Title." She currently resides in her childhood home on Long Island, New York.

www.ingramcontent.com/pod-product-compliance
Lightning Source LLC
Chambersburg PA
CBHW070809100426
42742CB00012B/2307